BLACK BLOCKS, WHITE SQUARES

LEONARD WILLIAMS

A
K

P
R
E
S
S

A crossword grid with numbered cells. Handwritten letters spell across the black squares: "BLACK", "BLOCKS", "WHITE", "SQUARES".

AK Press

370 Ryan Avenue #100

Chico, CA 95973

USA

www.akpress.org

akpress@akpress.org

AK Press

33 Tower Street

Edinburgh, EH6, 7BN

Scotland

www.akuk.com

akuk@akpress.org

Please contact us to request the latest AK Press distribution catalog, which features books, pamphlets, zines, and stylish apparel published and/or distributed by AK Press. Alternatively, visit our websites for the complete catalog, latest news, and secure ordering.

Cover and interior design by Crisis

Printed in the United States of America on acid-free paper

CONTENTS

For some years now, the notion of constructing politically themed crosswords seemed to be far-fetched. Friends would often ask if my academic interests in anarchist thought and radical politics would ever find a way into the crosswords I construct as an occasional contributor to national newspapers. Having the two worlds intersect rarely seemed possible—academic life was one thing; crossword construction was quite another.

However, new developments in those respective worlds have made a fruitful combination both possible and necessary. Renewed energy and dynamism in the streets, related to Black Lives Matter and anti-fascist efforts, provided the political spark. Progressive efforts among cruciverbalists to promote diverse voices and social justice causes (for example, projects such as Women of Letters, Queer Crosswords, Inkubator Crosswords, and Grids for Good) encouraged me to think about crosswords as a viable form of outreach and education. The result is this book of puzzles that highlights the political ideas, history, movements, and practices of anarchists and other radicals.

My fascination with words, language, and other symbols began when I was just coming into my teenage years. Dictionary discoveries, comedy and satire on television and in magazines, and debates in the news concerning civil rights and other causes captivated my attention. University studies in politics and philosophy, as well as literature and film, merely deepened those interests.

Political and social ideas soon became the primary vehicle for me to engage with language and understand its relationship to theory and practice. Student and antiwar activism co-existed with academic studies of political theory and ideologies. Those academic studies began with undergraduate papers on thinkers such as Marx, Augustine, and Bakunin. From there, I moved on to a master's thesis about the syndicalism of Georges Sorel and eventually a dissertation on the empirical study of ideologies within political science. After decades of writing on various topics for both academic and public audiences, I returned to thinking about anarchism after the so-called Battle of Seattle. The radicalism of that era inspired me to spend the remainder of my academic career studying anarchist theory and practice.

My connection with crossword puzzles can be traced to my stepfather, the son of Polish immigrants to the US, who had begun solving crosswords in local newspapers largely to improve his English vocabulary. I picked up this interest in crosswords from him, although my solving habit was intermittent until I entered graduate school. I then found that crosswords in local papers, the Sunday *New York Times*, and *Games* magazine provided welcome respite from the rigors of study. While writing my dissertation, I was inspired by the pleasures of solving crosswords to try my hand at creating a puzzle the old-fashioned way—using paper and pencil to lay out and fill a grid. That effort did not go at all well … but beginning in 2000, I happily discovered Cruciverb.com and Crossword Compiler software, and soon began publishing puzzles in major outlets.

Once again, this book of puzzles on anarchist and radical themes emerged as one way of combining career and hobby, vocation and avocation … bringing it all back home, so to speak. My aim was to shine a light on a significant number of ideas, practices, and orientations found within contemporary anarchism in the United States. It was impossible to cover every strain of ideological thought or every form of activist practice, but I believe that the collection has something for everyone.

The crosswords presented here were not intended for mainstream newspapers, although some themes could work in those outlets, but they were constructed with conventional standards in mind. The themes employed often use styles of wordplay (even some grid art) that solvers would find in typical crosswords. Some of the crosswords in the collection follow the rules and perhaps some even challenge them. Solvers can find creative themes that illustrate an idea or practice, rather than merely allude to it—following the maxim that a writer should "show" rather than "tell" the reader about the subject at hand. At times, though, I had to use a straightforward, didactic approach to develop the grids—for example, using illustrative quotations, invocations of important thinkers and books, or allusions to keywords and concepts.

As you work through the book, you will find some relatively easy puzzles and some relatively hard ones. Your experience and skill as a solver will determine which crosswords fall into which category, but I have appended a set of Constructor's Notes that rate the puzzles based on the theme type and on reactions from the test solvers. The Constructor's Notes also provide some background or commentary on the theme. If you get stuck while solving any individual puzzle, you might even find a hint to its solution in the Notes.

These crossword puzzles are designed to offer diversion with a purpose. Solve, Discover, and Learn. Have fun along the way!

ACKNOWLEDGMENTS

This book would not have been appeared, much less attempted, without substantial encouragement and support from others. Neil Wollman, my long-time friend and collaborator, was among the most persistent in encouraging me to think about blending the political and the cruciverbal. During the preparation of an academic volume on key concepts in anarchist thought, Laura Portwood-Stacer and I discovered our mutual interest in crosswords. She was the first person to learn of the idea for this work, and her guidance and advice made the project seem viable. Other scholars of anarchism also lent their voices in support of the project. Finally, Benjamin Tausig, renowned editor of the American Values Club crossword, and noted constructor Natan Last provided significant support and reassurance that the project would be worthwhile.

The debt of gratitude I owe to Lynne Flora Margolies—my friend, colleague, and birthday buddy—is immense, if not infinite. She tested more than half of the puzzles in the collection, making helpful comments on themes and clues that greatly improved each crossword. Lynne's love of language and crosswords is unmatched by anyone else I know, and her affinity for radical politics made her an ideal partner in this effort. She found joy in each new construction, and she kept my spirits up through the endless months of compiling the collection in stressful times. *Muchas gracias, mi amiga.*

Many thanks, too, to the many folks who volunteered to test solve one or more puzzles. Some of the test solvers were longstanding friends who like crosswords, while others were members of the Crossword Puzzle Collaboration Directory group on Facebook. Their attention to detail and candid feedback highlighted confusing clues, problematic fill, and themes that did not work. My profound thanks to all the test solvers: Michelle Calka, Kathy Davis, Katja Brinck, Derek Allen, Jeff Eddings, Kevin Lumpkin, Mark McClain, Jennifer Marra, and several others who preferred to remain anonymous. Rest assured, the blame for any remaining defects in the puzzles certainly rests solely with me and not with any of these fine people.

I must also thank the people at AK Press who not only agreed to publish this work, but whose many fine books have deeply enriched my understanding of anarchism. Thanks, too, to the many friends and colleagues who have supported, contributed to, and indulged my passions ... whether for studying ideologies and anarchism or for solving and constructing crossword puzzles. Special shout outs to my sons, Jason and Christopher, who often solve my published puzzles, and to my grandsons, Isaac and Harrison, who have shown some fascination with the work of constructing and solving puzzles. May they all continue the solving habit in the years to come. Most notably, no element of this project would be possible or meaningful without the love and support of my dearest Vicky, who continues to enrich my life beyond measure.

BLACK BLOCKS, WHITE SQUARES

GENERAL STRIKE

ACROSS

1 Counter sight, often
7 ___ Prof.
11 Modem rate abbr.
14 Lionel Richie hit of 1983
15 Poi root
16 Porridge grain
17 Community media outlet?
19 ___ Rida ("Low" performer)
20 Superman's leader?
21 Lobe location
22 Bid on eBay
24 Where you watch the soaps?
28 ___ corpus
31 Lift, in a way
32 Bakery finishers
33 University grad
35 Hockey legend Phil, for short
39 Appointment with your family doctor?
42 Annual presidential address, briefly
43 Pre-med hurdle
44 Convention accomodation
45 Do a longshoreman's job
47 Full of spunk
48 Where UN delegates play Big Ten basketball?
53 Doesn't pass the fact check
54 No longer in the closet
55 UN workers' agency
58 Dr. of rap
59 Small business loan?
64 Mens ___ (legal intent)
65 "That's enough! I get it!"
66 Elsewhere
67 Tundra denizen
68 Part of TAZ
69 Links

DOWN

1 Ilk
2 Promissory notes
3 Watering holes
4 Tokyo-bound carrier
5 Shapiro heard on NPR
6 Break in the school day
7 Video game pioneer
8 Morose
9 ___ Lanka
10 Past one's prime
11 Quaint praise for a show
12 Basic diet
13 Marvel mutant
18 H. ___ Brown ('60s radical)
23 Antislavery party of the 19th century
24 Greek hero
25 Beer-making oven
26 Affinity bond
27 Je t'___
28 Body parts that might get replaced
29 Phobia prefix
30 Rhythm
33 Pedal in car: Abbr.
34 Pastureland
36 Gains a lap
37 Audre Lorde, e.g.
38 Like a child without siblings
40 Film trivia site
41 Author Silverstein
46 Israeli novelist
47 Capitalist bigwig
48 Gorz who authored *A Strategy for Labor*
49 Syndicalist who mused about a relevant "myth"
50 No meal for a vegan
51 Radiohead frontman Thom
52 Vietnamese port
55 Roman calendar entry
56 Dryer trap contents
57 Eight in Roma
60 Boxing match result
61 Suffix with "ball" or "bass"
62 Hitter's stat
63 Linguistic suffix

INTERSECTIONALITY

We believe that sexual politics under patriarchy is as pervasive in Black women's lives as are the politics of class and race. We also often find it difficult to separate race from class from sex oppression because in our lives they are most often experienced simultaneously. —Combahee River Collective Statement (1977)

ACROSS

1 Critter catcher
5 Applaud
9 Ford Taurus, say
14 ___ of Moms (Portland protest tactic)
15 Cork location
16 *The Rights of Man* author
17 Cold treat
18 Mosquito repellant
19 Remove from the board
20 Many boomers
23 Overdone, in a way
24 Doc for a Spider-Man
25 Pipe type: Abbr.
28 Atlanta-to-Miami dir.
29 To wit
33 ___ *101* (Nickolodeon sitcom)
34 A Musketeer
35 Social customs
36 Works by Jacques-Louis David, e.g.
41 Vacuous
42 Course guaranteed to boost your GPA
43 Iowa State city
44 Fastener needing a lug wrench
46 Loop transport grp.
49 Amy who wrote *The Joy Luck Club*
50 Director Anderson
51 Freud colleague
53 Actress Kelly, in Monaco
58 Styling spot
60 Each, colloquially
61 "___ ecological society possible?'
62 Hopping mad
63 Tuscan city with a noted university (and a tower)
64 This: Sp.
65 Patron saint of Paris
66 Dismal sci.
67 Tie-___ (adds color to a plain white tee)

DOWN

1 Some soft serve cones
2 Indy cars, say
3 Author of *Reservation Blues*
4 Fabric fold
5 Formally turn over
6 Mortgage claim
7 For a rectangle, it's l × w
8 Gasoline in Gloucestershire
9 Word before a woof
10 Merit, as an award
11 Dispersion of a people
12 Quiz response: Abbr.
13 Maiden name indicator
21 How to approach some topics
22 Quite aloof
26 Turn suddenly
27 Dermatological concern
30 "I get it now!"
31 ___ def (certainly)
32 Thames estuary locale
33 Advocate for Dreyfus
34 Does something
35 Big name in appliances
36 Prim and proper
37 *Clueless* source material
38 Residential layout
39 LOTR actor McKellen
40 Syst. with a Bakersfield campus
44 Rooster?
45 Ford SUV
46 Stay ___ San Diego (Ron Burgundy meme)
47 Mexican pale lager
48 United Center and Staples Center
50 Cabs, say
52 Cut partner
54 Indian flatbread
55 Failure descriptor
56 Meh
57 Bridge
58 Comedy legend Caesar
59 Word between you and here

1	2	3	4	■	5	6	7	8	■	9	10	11	12	13
14				■	15				■	16				
17				■	18				■	19				
20				21					22				■	■
23					■	■		24			■	25	26	27
28			■	29	30	31	32			■	33			
■	■	■	34					■	■	35				
36	37	38						39	40					
41					■	■	42					■	■	■
43				■	44	45					■	46	47	48
49			■	50			■	■	■	51	52			
■	■	53	54				55	56	57					
58	59				■	60				■	61			
62					■	63				■	64			
65					■	66				■	67			

5

HAVEN

SPACE OF ESCAPE FROM THE STATE

ACROSS

1 Host of *The Gist* podcast
6 ___ Against the Machine
10 Dieter's concern
14 Les jeunes filles, par exemple
15 Kazan who ratted on Hollywood comrades
16 Author of *A Death in the Family*
17 Reluctant (to)
18 Ideologue's attitude, say
20 With 36-, 39-, and 50-Across, a certain haven
22 *Hair* co-creator
23 Wee, alternatively
24 ___ pants
27 Whole
32 What a Zamboni maintains
33 Not stained
36 See 20-Across
38 Lesley of *60 Minutes* fame
39 See 20-Across
40 Coordinated
42 *Delta of Venus* author
43 Tempest location, possibly
44 Shouts of "Bravo!"
47 Feel regret for
49 Dies ___ (hymn)
50 See 20-Across
56 Overlapping dialogue
57 Rashida of "The Squad" in Congress
59 Interstate traveler
60 Otherwise
61 Barista's creation
62 Camisoles, say
63 Inoperative, as an engine
64 Test format

DOWN

1 Education grant eponym
2 Beings in an H. G. Wells novel
3 Butcher's unit
4 Et ___ (and so forth)
5 Yoga retreat location
6 Verso's opposite
7 Away from the wind
8 Prepares or secures
9 Consume some carryout
10 Blanchett who portrayed Schlafly
11 Arroyo fill, in Spanish
12 Have another go
13 Point of contention
19 Tehran resident, most likely
21 Toothpaste endorser: Abbr.
24 Captain in a cockpit
25 Not ___ in the world
26 Popular game for constructors?
28 Explosive network?
29 Turner autobiography
30 Send a payment
31 Heavenly havens
33 Snack food brand
34 When doubled, Silentó's dance move
35 An advanced degree
37 Giving ___ (greeting, in a way)
38 Located
41 Social conventions
44 Stretch of history
45 Range rovers
46 Actresses George and Arcieri
48 Of the same status: Fr.
49 Signed
50 Double Stuf brand
51 Antic comedy
52 Divine mother of the pharaoh
53 Iconic *Casablanca* role
54 Cereal grain
55 Silent film star Naldi
56 Ill. setting in winter
58 Hakim ___, whose ideas are reflected in this puzzle

1	2	3	4	5	■	6	7	8	9	■	10	11	12	13
14					■	15				■	16			
17					■	18				19				
20					21									
■	■	■	22				■	23			■	■	■	■
24	25	26				■	■				28	29	30	31
32			■			33	34	35						
36			37	■	38					■	39			
40									■	■			42	
43						■		44	45	46				
■	■	■	■	47		48		49			■	■	■	■
■	50	51	52				53					54	55	■
56									■	57				58
59				■	60				■	61				
62				■	63				■	64				

7

ACROSS

1 Emmy-winning talk show host Tyler
6 His sentence commuted on 11/10/1887; pardoned on 6/26/1893
12 Out of the wind, nautically
16 ___ This Book (Abbie Hoffman work)
17 Russian threesome
18 Advance a petition's cause
19 The cause (May 1886)
21 Hiccup
22 The A. in A. Philip Randolph
23 One of Saturn's moons
24 Journalist's concern
25 Org. opposed to speciesism
26 Promises not to tell: Abbr.
29 Come together
30 With 62-Across, last words for one of the martyrs (15-Down)
35 Smart speaker brand
37 Grp. opposed to white supremacy and colonialism
38 Inexperienced with
40 Party host's request
44 Sappho's P
45 He was martyred on 11/11/1887
49 Not well lit
50 Coppers
51 Chiwere-speaking tribe
52 Bed-Ins for Peace participant
53 He was martyred on 11/11/1887 (founder of the International Working People's Association)
56 Daily grind, e.g.
57 Fish and chips side
58 Unit of gentrification
59 Suit to ___
60 Marcuse's ___ and Civilization
62 See 30-Across
66 Identity theft target: Abbr.
69 Home to Iowa State
71 Some Iowa State Fair sounds
72 What the faithful practice
74 Perform, as a task
77 Seal scion
80 Produit de la tête
81 The anthem sung on 11/11/1887
84 Noted island of exile
85 Reptile in a Tennessee Williams title
86 Playwright Henrik
87 Search for
88 Fielden, whose sentence was commuted on 11/10/1887 and who was pardoned on 6/26/1893
89 Program interruptions

DOWN

1 Sailing
2 "How Sweet __ To Be Loved By You" (Marvin Gaye song)
3 Video game company
4 Scoffer's interjection
5 Tennis star Gibson
6 Minnesota college
7 Mötley ___
8 Automotive noisemaker
9 Enlarge, as a highway
10 Alias indicator: Abbr.
11 San Francisco, say
12 Org.
13 He committed suicide while in jail
14 Equal, in Evian
15 He was martyred on 11/11/1887
20 Hebrew letter
24 Bat wood
25 ROC antagonist
27 Unmoved by, as an appeal
28 Demo, possibly
30 ___ nails
31 Like many a climb
32 Automated vacuum
33 Like a museum piece, sometimes
34 Workout unit
36 LOTR creature
39 ___ first (Abbott & Costello bit)
41 What Indiana has, but Iowa doesn't?
42 Convention centers, e.g.
43 Like Senate presidents, often
45 Start of the second qtr.
46 Silicon Valley enterprise
47 Take a stand against
48 Hers: Fr.
54 Maternal sheep
55 Old nutritional concern: Abbr.
59 Sounds of relief
61 Sunbeam
63 Location for many talk radio shows
64 Islamic unit of weight
65 Stop that!
66 He was martyred on 11/11/1887, after saying "The time will come when our silence will be more powerful than the voices you strangle today."
67 Approach furtively
68 He was sentenced to prison; pardoned on 6/26/1893
70 Play a ukulele
73 Furniture wood
75 Brother of Jacob
76 State bird of Hawaii
77 Leaning tower city
78 Like thrift store items
79 Writing implements
81 Chief leader?
82 ___ Khan
83 IPA stat

AFFINITY GROUP

ACROSS

1 Spat
5 Diner dessert
13 Indigenous people of the Mountain West
16 Guthrie of folk music
17 Seagoing staple, once
18 Airline to Stockholm
19 Document cited in *The Big Bang Theory*
22 WBUR talk show
23 La ___ Méditerranée
24 Annapolis inst.
25 Instructional phase
27 Quite capable
29 It's seen at a reunion
36 Catherine of *Schitt's Creek*
37 Start of a lunar month
38 Win a Powerball jackpot
41 Magma on a mountain
42 Pirelli product for an Aston Martin
46 UK clock setting
47 Academic administrator
49 Evening, in ad copy
51 Batteries for many toys
52 River in Flanders
54 Where stocks trade: Abbr.
56 Sandwich go-with?
58 Regards highly
61 Muppet with a striped shirt
62 Troubleshooting concern
67 Terry McMillan novel, *Waiting to ___*
68 Bouncy rhythm
69 Comforting kitten sound
70 ___ bono? (who benefits?)
73 Joins the class roster
78 Group for grads
82 Some COs
83 Vikings
84 Andean people
85 Sorta
86 Shot at a café
87 Not attend, as a class

DOWN

1 Pacific root vegetable
2 Fe (symbolically)
3 Movie that just didn't make it
4 Worry about missing the party: Abbr.
5 Song for a sea voyage: Var.
6 Sealyham Terrier, say
7 Before in verse
8 Comedic Sandler
9 Long-term loan: Abbr.
10 Surname in *The Incredibles*
11 Frozen part of a margarita
12 Barely manage (by)
13 Applies to
14 Wine acid
15 Country house and grounds
20 Seemingly lost
21 Wolverine, say
26 Sharpie product
27 WWII maritime menaces
28 West Bank grp.
29 Like summer days on the Golden Gate Bridge
30 Throat-clearing sounds
31 Non-glossy finish
32 Like some outlet store merch
33 Nice seasoning
34 Actor McGregor of *Trainspotting*
35 Roman 2007
39 ___ Pompidou (Parisian art museum)
40 Kahlo portrayer
43 Greek composer
44 Early broadcast medium
45 German steel city
48 Very brief moment: Abbr.
50 Euripides tragedy
53 Heat up again, as leftovers
55 Fall Out Boy pop genre
57 Studio product
59 Our Sun
60 Ego Nwodim show, briefly
62 Like the Sherpa
63 Finds joy (in)
64 Robin's relative
65 Your sister's daughters
66 Inlfuential weather phenomenon
70 Bottom-feeding fish
71 Cold War abbr.
72 Words of understanding
74 Redding in the Rock Hall of Fame
75 Clickable text on a Web page
76 Scenes
77 Lose it
79 St. Louis-to-Chicago dir.
80 Apple platform
81 Meditative sounds

DIRECT ACTION

ACROSS

1 Accumulate
6 Epic fail
12 Org. for the 50+
16 Maine's ___ Bay
17 Knows about, as a conspiracy
18 Trade org. certifying gold albums
19 Part 1 of a definition
21 Assns.
22 Scarcity
23 ___ button issue
24 Insects in cocoons
25 Eye trouble
26 Part 2 of the definition
29 Tabula ___
31 Middling grade
32 Karel Capek scifi play
33 Crude commodity
36 Restaurant handout
38 Submerged civilization in myth
40 Part 3 of the definition
43 Summer drink suffix
44 Wise one
45 Rosa of civil rights fame
47 Exclamation of sadness
51 Peri's role on *Frasier*
54 Part 4 of the definition
57 He played Harvey Milk
61 UK lexicons
62 Full-contact combat: Abbr.
63 Bus. tel. no.
64 Anger
65 Partakes, in a posh manner
67 Final part of the definition
72 2019 World Series champs
76 ___ *of Two Cities*
77 Cat in Castille
78 Experienced hand
80 US poet laureate Dove
81 Author of *Direct Action: An Ethnography*
83 Folder on a screen
84 Audrey Tautou movie of 2001
85 Venerated one
86 Performed in an opera
87 Surgically remove
88 Anti-Stalinists

DOWN

1 Corrosive liquids
2 Painter of *The Absinthe Drinker*
3 Analyze chemically
4 Runner who makes it home
5 Like fine cotton
6 Evergreen
7 Scifi writer Asimov
8 Emmy-winning Tyler
9 Mind another's business
10 Send an email to
11 4/4
12 Have it out, in words
13 Armstrong or O'Hare
14 Home of the Moai statues
15 Quarterbacks, say
20 "It makes sense now."
24 Make a case
27 NYSE index
28 Lugosi of horror films
30 Letters on many black churches
33 Photo ___
34 One way to save for the future: Abbr.
35 Forest sight
37 Sprinting Bolt
38 Invite
39 Well-trimmed
41 Builder of the Large Hadron Collider: Abbr.
42 Comic bark
46 Throws off
48 Take it on the ___ (flee)
49 Box o' bills
50 Caspian or Caribbean
52 Offer one's views
53 Hero's opposite
55 Trimmer?
56 Target of identity theft: Abbr.
57 Humorist David or Amy
58 Curiosities
59 Really pigged out
60 Approach to tennis play
66 Cause to be loved
68 Colloquialisms
69 Overhangs
70 8-point item in a Scrabble set
71 ___ acid (disinfectant)
73 Class for an able HS sr.
74 Reznor of Nine Inch Nails
75 Classifies
79 Persist
81 ___ es Salaam (Tanzanian seaport)
82 Acquire

WHY THE BLACK FLAG?

COLOR SYMBOLISM

ACROSS

1 Bug in the system
6 Wedding vows
10 *Republic* author
15 Big name in cubes
16 Path to navigate
18 Tanker from the Gulf
19 "Would you like to see ___?"
20 Moved like The Blob
21 Yemeni neighbor
22 Miami Heat all-star
25 Amiri Baraka, né ___ Jones
26 Greek society letter
27 Logical principle
33 Bert's pal on the Street
34 United
35 Wrinkled citrus fruits
39 Comic-Con attendee
40 Dad jokes, e.g.
44 Hardware store chain
45 Martinique, par exemple
46 Like some writers
47 Dover locale: Abbr.
48 Speedway curve, phonetically
49 Greek wines
50 Pharmaceutical container
51 Coarse hairs
53 Had a bite
54 Have more than a bite
55 Source of some distress
60 NYC transit co.
61 How to serve a Reuben
62 Notable rose
68 Vinyl playing option
69 Pale purple
70 Jah believer
74 *And Still ___* (Angelou work)
75 Providentially fortunate
76 Lost one's way
77 Fraternal name in Americana
78 Breyer's competitor
79 Pares and improves

DOWN

1 Mrs. in Monterrey
2 ___ lock key
3 Simpson or Lincoln
4 Auction winner
5 Lanai strings
6 Like some patches
7 Lulu
8 Anise-flavored liqueur
9 21st educational focus
10 Free Parking space, once
11 Sketching, in a way
12 Jai ___
13 Miss. neighbor
14 Source for a copy: Abbr.
17 Early name for Tokyo
23 Mine find
24 Global news source: Abbr.
27 Gainsays
28 Words implying a threat
29 Protest, to the authorities
30 Net protectors
31 UN Secretary General Kofi ___
32 Brandon ___ (Hilary Swank's *Boys Don't Cry* role)
36 Dockworker's job
37 Mammoth cartoon
38 Vendor
40 Prereq for a PhD
41 Fix a paved road
42 Brasil a Chile dirección
43 Some cars: Abbr.
46 Dalai Lama's cause
50 Napa Valley site
52 Sofa part
54 Laurel
56 Source of campaign funds: Abbr.
57 "Piece of cake!"
58 Passes, as a statute
59 ___ Hill (Sisqo's original group)
62 Gobi Desert setting
63 Weapon with many warheads
64 Actress Falco
65 Priestly vestment
66 River dammed at Aswan
67 Ran, as colors
71 Hindu honorific
72 Lunar new year
73 Spots for candidates

MUTUAL AID

LENDING A HAND ... BEFORE AND AFTER

ACROSS

1 Makes a lap
5 Biblical song
10 Where Samson fought the Philistines
14 Dolphinfish, for short
15 Suffix indicating pain
16 Neuron fiber
17 Meteor streak, once
18 "Cope!" or cope
20 Socks that stay up in the ER?
22 RAF medal
23 *Almost Famous* Hudson
24 European finch
25 ___ retirement
27 Coleridge's "Dejection"
29 Blast material: Abbr.
30 Puerto ___
31 Inert Calder
35 GPS element for folks seeking forgiveness?
39 Seville and Mandarin
40 Flanged fastener
42 Pro
45 Sunrise direction, in Saxony
46 Warrior pose, say
47 ___ of faith
49 Squad member from Minnesota
52 Part of some rapper names
53 Busy place for caterers on Thanksgiving Day?
57 West African nation
58 Phil who sang "Love Me, I'm a Liberal"
59 Memphis river
60 Ride
61 Never mind the dele
62 Flits
63 Sign of a broadcast
64 Source of petrol in Canada

DOWN

1 Slow burn
2 1971 Neil Diamond hit
3 Power of *Star Wars*
4 Trigonometry ratio
5 Where Galileo lectured
6 Was out for the night
7 Visibly in awe
8 Friend of Stitch
9 Bryn ___
10 Turning tool
11 Make a strong appeal
12 Sauce for potstickers
13 Motive
19 Being-in-___ (Sartre)
21 Word before high or blue
26 Wolf
27 Theatre award
28 Rick Wilson's *Everything Trump Touches* ___
31 Mmes. in Madrid
32 Camper's shelter
33 Prelude to trig.
34 Some first-responders: Abbr.
36 Memento of success
37 Confucian classic
38 Beats soundly
41 Has a conversation with
42 Putting on an act
43 Colman of *The Crown*
44 Like a classic dad joke
46 Dadaist who worked in torn paper
48 Expanse of farmland
49 Catherine of *Schitt's Creek*
50 Footballer who's earned six Ballon d'Or awards
51 Modify, as a recipe
54 Reverberate
55 Midday
56 One a day, say

SOLUTION: 116, BOTTOM RIGHT

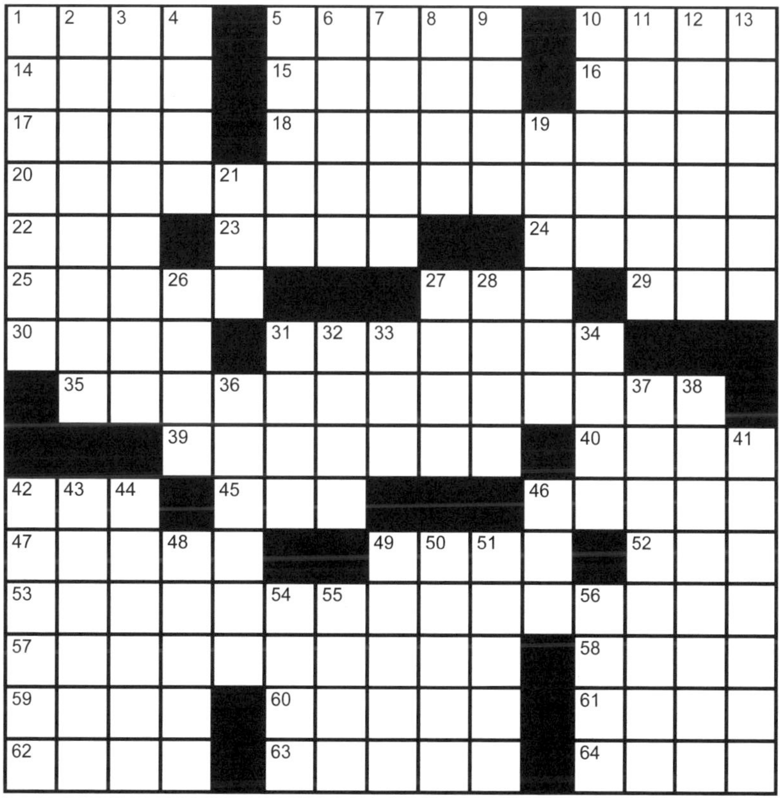

CAPITALIST PYRAMID

Drawn from an illustration in the Industrial Worker *(1911)*

ACROSS

1 Typesetter's measure
5 Oscar, in *The Odd Couple*
9 Neighborhood of Lower Manhattan
13 Ark builder
17 It's equal to eight ounces
18 Piece of cake
19 Pond swimmer
20 Iberian river
21 Monarchs and politicians say . . .
23 Office assistant
25 Seattle's summertime setting: Abbr.
26 Chats, electronically
27 Preachers and teachers say . . .
28 Crack units
30 Not keep up
33 Continent south of Eur.
34 Tinder abbr.
35 The military says . . .
39 Agricultural org. for teens
41 More than satisfy, like a meal
42 Harrison song on *Let It Be*
44 Bear genus
48 With hands on hips
51 Subdivision units
53 ___ *Jury* (Mickey Spillane novel)
54 Grammy-winner for *Invasion of Privacy* (2018)
57 ___ date
59 Minnesota metro area
61 Lawyers org.

62 The bourgeoisie says . . .
66 Flatow of *Science Friday*
67 Noted Ottawa chief
69 Due follower
70 Diagnostic procedure
72 Not well behaved
73 Catcher's possession
76 Roust
78 Molecule components
80 Sites for spelunkers
82 Et ___
86 Cooking spray name
88 The proletariat says . . .
91 "Either you do it, ___ will!"
94 Once around the track
96 Eastbound destination from SFO, maybe
97 Enduring
98 The peasants say . . .
102 Copier abbr.
103 Type of concert merch
104 Well-known Fleetwood Mac song
105 Woodstock Nation symbol
108 Noted English boarding school
109 About, in legalese
110 Gumbo ingredient
111 Chum
112 "See you!"
113 Eleanor's successor
114 Noodge
115 Pay to play

DOWN

1 Yellowish fruits
2 Soda alternative

3 Most abrupt
4 *The Problem With* ___ (Hari Kondabolu's documentary)
5 Appear to be true
6 Brand of chips
7 ___ negro (black bear)
8 Provo inst.
9 Warning about a link
10 Scrape, to a kid
11 ___ loaf . . .
12 Singular event
13 Little ___ (Dickens character)
14 Toes the line
15 Equipment for an archer
16 Snake oil
22 Prom rental
24 Setting for Gerald Durrell's *My Family and Other Animals*
29 Leading the pack
30 Correlation coefficient named for a Greek letter
31 Stopped by a diner
32 Place to train
36 Director Robbins
37 Cruet's contents
38 Game with Skip cards
40 Seed cover
43 Online site for crafts
45 Marcus Aurelius, e.g.
46 Communications officer on the Enterprise
47 Enterprise offering
49 Fuzzy fruit
50 Construction girder
52 Soup starter
54 Film director synonymous with Americana

55 Circa
56 Unknown person, in slang
58 Elder newt
60 Like most puppy pics
63 Vaping instrument, briefly
64 Barack Obama, for one
65 Use another phrase
68 Do a short-term job
71 Kit component
74 Credit checker Experian, formerly
75 Lower digit
77 Post or pose a question
79 Marketing
81 Even prime
83 Native of Vientiane
84 Not at all kosher
85 Pasta preference
87 Fill-in-the-blank story template
89 One-percenter
90 Scary one in a fairy tale
91 Young bird of prey
92 Vaquero's lariat
93 ___ now, when?
95 *The Rights of Man* author
99 Mother of Tracy in *Hairspray*
100 POTUS and the Speaker, say
101 Brand with a famous recipe
102 Ryan Gosling film, ___ *and the Real Girl* (2007)
105 Soda, to some
106 ___ out a living (get by)
107 Administrator of 2020's PPP

CIVILIZATION AND ITS DISCONTENTS

ACROSS

1 Need some relief
5 Nero's 902
9 Neighborhood informants?
16 Hotspot offering
18 The mid-Atlantic, say
19 Problematic product
20 Personal injury attorney, at times
21 Fab
22 Van Gogh's village
24 Cape Cod community
25 Triple ___ (liqueur)
27 Result of wage labor
29 Darjeeling drink
32 Joey in Milne's stories
34 Genetic polymer
35 Comfortably cozy
36 Manufacturing
39 Trim a lawn
41 Certain sports cars: Abbr.
42 Hardness scale eponym
43 Where to plant plants
45 Appropriate for the occasion
47 Taming
53 Ride
54 Make like a cat
55 Part of a Hunter S. Thompson title
58 Dosage datum: Abbr.
61 One of three teams for King James
64 Communication medium
67 "___ my guard down" (words of regret)
69 Bit of ink
70 Legislator's roll-call vote
71 Satirical folkie Lehrer
72 Combines and computers, for example
76 Diner favorite
78 Sideshow
79 Ghostly Marley
81 Ethernet and USB
85 Bob Marley standard
87 Social order
89 Baltic country
90 Dik-diks and kudus
91 What a squirrel does to a tree
92 Won a bout, in a way: Abbr.
93 Countermand a dele

DOWN

1 Elementary principles
2 Apsáalooke people residing in Montana
3 Where a batter starts
4 Industrial designers Charles and Ray
5 Hemp-derived oil: Abbr.
6 Goddess of rebirth
7 Prefix to mural
8 Goethe's "Hermann and Dorothea," e.g.
9 Welcome boon
10 "And when I ___ my lips, let no dog bark!" (Shakespeare)
11 Phila. transit system
12 Quick ones, in a bar
13 Sending forth
14 Look from an upstairs window
15 Some wraps
17 Indulgent grandparents
23 Limerick land
26 Camper's resting place
28 Bother persistently
29 "There are some who call me . . . ___"
30 Grammy-winning producer Brian
31 Adderall is prescribed for it
33 Symbols of royal power
37 Org. with quadrennial trials
38 So far
40 Start to cycle?
44 Vague, as a memory
46 Stir fry curd
48 Air or Pro
49 Laureate's inspiration
50 Collectible from Disney's *Alice Solves the Puzzle*
51 Home antonym
52 Without clutter
56 Not long ___ (recently)
57 *Automatic for the People* band
58 Maker of the C3 Pluriel
59 Detox
60 Things to keep
62 Hugo hero
63 Walkway in ancient Greece
65 Kans. neighbor
66 Gayle to Oprah
68 Everything else
73 Blinding colors
74 Onetime messaging service
75 Grab, in slang
77 Some mowers
80 Opponent of Bernie and Kamala, once
82 Paper for a purchase: Abbr.
83 Quaker pronoun
84 Part of iOS: Abbr.
86 Sundial figure
88 ___ state

PREFIGURATIVE POLITICS

UNITY OF MEANS AND ENDS

ACROSS

1 Ingrid's role in *Casablanca*
5 Largest of the Inner Hebrides
9 What teachers and students share
14 Agts.
15 Complement of socks
16 Himalayan humanoids
17 Doing the right thing (means to 59-Across)
20 ___ for Fears (1980s band)
21 Walk, as through puddles
22 Big name in early science fiction
23 Universal agreement (means to 52-Across)
27 Guru's title
28 NBA Hall of Famer Patrick
30 Mideast federation: Abbr.
31 Claiming a space (means to 41-Across)
34 ___-up (suppressed)
35 Barrett of Pink Floyd
36 "Gotcha!"
38 Agricultural unit
41 Mutual support (end of 31-Across)
48 Torero's encouragement
49 Co-author with Cloward of *Poor People's Movements*
50 Middling grade
51 Collective spirit (end of 24-Across)
55 Big name in tractors
57 *A Confederacy of Dunces* author
58 Aristotle's end
59 Freedom (end of 17-Across)
64 Nashville's Bridgestone
65 Actress Faris of *Scary Movie*
66 Lemon ___
67 1946 Nobelist in Literature
68 Fly high
69 Pretentiously cultured

DOWN

1 Choler
2 Start to complain?
3 Like a ball
4 Like the Uyghurs
5 Day ___
6 Penn of the Harold & Kumar series
7 Yorkie's woof
8 Go astray
9 Use a bike lane
10 Provide a hint
11 Subject to discussion
12 Spicy cuisine: Var.
13 Compass pt.
18 Like a haunted house
19 Beast of burden
22 Brandy bottle ltrs.
23 Op. ___
24 Japanese folklore baddie
25 Doctors Without Borders, e.g.
26 Word between "game" and "match"
29 Crumples, as a sheet of paper
32 Function
33 Roundabout, essentially
34 ___ favor
37 "Water Music" composer
38 Green New Deal proponent: Abbr.
39 Motion to end debate
40 Often misplaced devices
42 Nail polish brand that's a subsidiary of Coty
43 Eng. course
44 Brown, for one
45 Freeze, as a pond
46 Most direct
47 ___-haw!
52 Shows one's rude side?
53 Arm bones
54 Prefix for Platonist
56 *Hamilton* role for Phillipa Soo
58 Nicholas or Alexander
59 "Say ___"
60 Degrees en route to a Ph.D.
61 Fluxus movement artist, singer, activist
62 Article in Solidaridad Obrera?
63 Hog haven

ANTI-HIERARCHY

LET'S GIVE EVERYONE AN EVEN BREAK

ACROSS

1 Rainbows
5 Some retired professors
12 Fish for trout
16 *M*A*S*H* soda brand
17 Disparages, in slang
18 Ron Howard's breakout role
19 Fed, in noir films
20 Seismologist's scale
21 Tach figs.
22 Having good judgment
25 College in upstate NY
27 *Atonement* author McEwan
28 Spanish estuary
29 Ergonomic ride
35 Frat party activity
36 https://crimethinc.com, for example
37 Brand that emerged after breaking up a Rockefeller trust
39 Argentine tennis legend
40 Show the way
42 Toll road: Abbr.
43 Binary person
46 Secret society or its members

48 DiFranco of the Righteous Babe Foundation
49 ___-A-Sketch
52 Halt, nautically
54 Many an adopted dog
56 Craft brewery staple
57 Dried up
61 Group of global skeptics
64 Issue central to the *Mrs. America* plotline
65 Quit working
66 Puts up stakes
67 Doing it
73 Dating from
74 *Clue* suspect color
75 Sign for addl. authors
78 45 minutes of a soccer match
79 Cry of acclamation
80 ___ match
81 Nautical affirmatives
82 Requests a date
83 Swiss-born painter Paul

DOWN

1 With 77-Down, *Life of Pi* director

2 "Losing My Religion" band
3 Grail
4 Trig function graph
5 Honor, in Hamburg (anagram of "here")
6 Postal delivery
7 Some works by Albrecht Dürer
8 Microwave, say
9 Hagia Sophia locale
10 ___ the line (conformed)
11 Concerning, legally
12 Decorative molding
13 Entices
14 *The* ___ (video game)
15 Hardy character
23 Nosferatu, e.g.
24 Like a good wine, for many
25 Metro hub, briefly
26 Concert merch
30 Rodeo wear
31 Doe that fawned Faline
32 Wrath
33 Ingredient in a Bloody Caesar
34 *SportsCenter* channel
38 Signs off on

41 Viral video source, sometimes
43 Quiche Lorraine ingredient
44 Plenty, informally
45 Black Panther for Chadwick Boseman
47 He gave voice to Tom Joad
50 Source of tax help: Abbr.
51 Onerous duty
52 Colloquial "Never!"
53 Home opp. (on scoreboards)
55 Trade war tools
58 Check one's addition
59 Summertime along the Seine
60 Functional leader?
62 Spinning toon "devil"
63 Princess party swag
67 Sounds of laughter
68 Start of the US anthem
69 Dept. of Labor agency
70 Sgts., for example
71 Restaurant website section
72 Rat-___
76 Allow time to ferment
77 See 1-Down

ACROSS

1 *Doctor Who* venue
4 Exercise units
9 Settled a tab
13 Binary choice
15 "___ like to live dangerously" (Austin Powers)
16 Streaming service
17 Words of praise for the Earth?
20 Keeps from rocking
21 Somewhat pretentious
22 Ian who played Bilbo
23 Scotch accompaniment
25 Tribute band covering "The Middle"?
30 Girl from Glasgow
31 Attribute for a surgeon
33 DiFranco of Righteous Babe Records
34 Place to dwell
36 Hawaiian roll, e.g.
37 Desalination plant's input
40 DEA official
41 Sherlock Holmes case in which the Sovereign's Orb disappears?
45 Charged particles
46 Posse
47 Eat a cookie like a monster
50 Orientation request
54 Almost comatose (and truly so)?
57 Revealing glow
58 South Florida metropolis
59 Spelling or Amos
60 Ship's stabilizer
61 Fence entryways
62 Wii predecessor

DOWN

1 Tire store areas
2 Hiker's gear
3 Metal band Mötley ___
4 Island by the Strait of Messina
5 Start of a seventh-inning song
6 Trees lining the National Mall
7 Early K-pop idol
8 Soak up, in a way
9 Hatshepsut, for example
10 English for 56-Down
11 La Corse et Martinique
12 Deontological concern
14 Big name in lullabies
18 Baseball's Blue Moon
19 Serving spoon
23 Piercing ornament
24 Scary one in a fairy tale
25 Writer Evanovich
26 Thomas in the Basketball Hall of Fame
27 Of ___ (-ish)
28 Celesteville monarch
29 Accustom
30 ___ Vegas
32 Party org.
34 Deity for Akhenaten
35 Harry's first lady
38 Yankovic known for song parodies
39 Flying
40 Of the most recent vintage
42 Plot or ploy
43 Short summary
44 T'Challa, for example
47 Pierre locale, briefly
48 Opposite of alte
49 Alpine river
50 Question that reveals one wasn't paying attention
51 ___ Ra (Egyptian deity)
52 He created a "Utopia"
53 Partner of Osiris
55 Exclamation this side of "WTF"
56 Spanish for 10-Down

FROM MARGIN TO CENTER

ACROSS

1 Broadway choreographer for *Chicago*
6 Cared for a friend's pet
12 Large citrus fruits
19 Funds, in budget-speak
20 Equally simple
21 Clothing, at a Renaissance Faire
22 Resting one's eyes, say
23 Collection in which Audre Lorde observes that the master's tools won't dismantle the master's house
25 Some CBS procedurals
26 And others (often abbreviated bibliographic phrase)
27 Time of a Roman month
28 Item that was not burned in a 1960s protest
29 Famous refrain in a Sojourner Truth speech
32 ___, *A Lawyer in History* (biography of radical attorney Weinglass)
33 Shades of color
34 Ornamental shrub
35 So be it (literally)
37 ___ *of the City* (Maupin work)
38 ___ Cruces, New Mexico
39 Judith Butler's analysis of performativity
43 Beetle that once symbolized resurrection
47 Yoga poses
48 Choose (for)
49 Eagle's claw
50 1839 slave mutiny ship
52 Tenth-century start (old style)
53 Test score, often: Abbr.
56 Mary Wollstonecraft promotes education in ___ *of the Rights of Woman*
58 Sybilic
60 Latvian capital
61 Court dividers
62 Soup noodle
63 Go below the surface
64 Some states have legalized it
66 Book in which Simone de Beauvoir proclaims that "one is not born, but rather becomes, a woman"
70 *48* ___ (Eddie Murphy's film debut)
71 Tigers in a box score
72 Lions and tigers, not bears
73 West, in San Juan
74 Cheerios grain
75 Anne Rice's vampire
76 Tams' cousins
77 Work of radical rage by Valerie Solanas
81 NBA player in Dallas
82 Taboos
83 Tom Joad, for one
84 Portuguese "thanks"
89 Glom ___ (grab)
90 Canonized femme: Abbr.
91 Gloria Anzaldúa's exploration of *mestiza* consciousness
94 Charleston's state: Abbr.
95 Sandals bare them
96 "Remember the ___" (appeal from 65-Down)
97 Quran component
98 Kate Millett's radical feminist classic
101 Put on airs
103 Resistance to change
104 Schools, in Sancerre
105 Do more than get by
106 Eponymous figure for the anti-technological
107 Taxonomic groups
108 Reindeer relative

DOWN

1 Geological relic
2 One way to gamble
3 Midafternoon rest
4 Date
5 Sixth sense
6 Twin of Pollux
7 How you should take me, it's said
8 Vehicle that holds a charge
9 Audited, as a college class
10 Cruising
11 Norse god of war
12 Circumspect
13 Like some porridge
14 Have nostalgia for
15 UK recording label
16 Long-lasting source of light
17 Like many a silent film
18 Berlin street
19 Area known as "The Las Vegas of Asia"
24 Edmonton hockey team
26 Some bleaters
30 Amherst, relative to Boston
31 Small amount of ointment
33 ___ couture (high fashion)
35 Khashoggi involved in the Iran-Contra affair
36 Anthropologist author of *Coming of Age in Samoa*
37 Kind of sentence
39 Ways of walking
40 They: It.
41 Alliance with a phonetic alpahbet
42 Star of *Everybody Loves Raymond*
43 Corn ___ (thickener)
44 Roe served as an hors d'oeuvre
45 Trues, in carpentry
46 Saoirse of *Lady Bird*
50 Perform well on, as a test
51 Wrestling match requisites
52 Often-derided shoe brand
53 Puckered fabric
54 Dick of late-night TV fame
55 Kids' favorite dinos
57 Available as a trial version
58 River on the Polish-German border
59 Milk dispenser
62 Avail
65 Abigail who made the appeal on behalf of 96-Across
66 Nothing ___ here . . .
67 Porkpies and fedoras
68 Part of QED
69 ". . . I will fear ___" (Psalm 23)
72 Modify a mortgage, briefly
74 Melville novel that's a crossword staple
75 Here's how it's done
76 Star fired from a 2018 sitcom reboot
77 Strands during the winter
78 Come together
79 Free of duty
80 Jotting place
81 All the Beatles received them: Abbr.
84 Steps scene in Eisenstein's *Potemkin*

SOLUTION: 118, TOP RIGHT

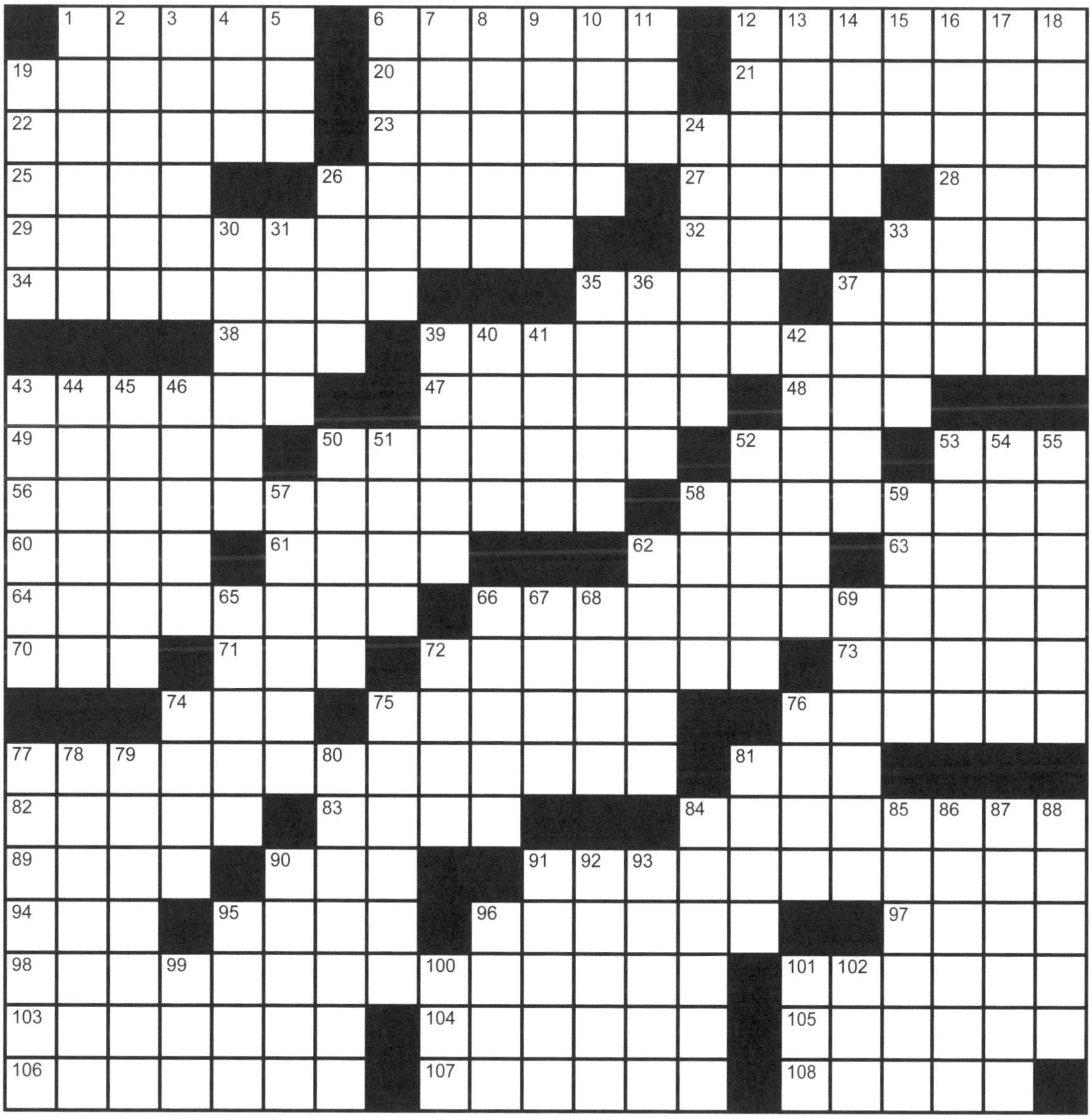

85 Pub prefix
86 Underworld god with a canine head
87 Start of an automotive mnemonic, possibly
88 Tribe known indigenously as Wazhazhe
90 Sphere, e.g.
91 Conductor's "instrument"
92 Swan Lake role
93 Kitchen tool resembling a garlic press
95 __ *carreta* (giant armadillo)
96 Head __ (problem for school-aged children)
99 www.akpress.org, for example
100 Relay stage
101 Cashpoint, in the US
102 Funny Margaret

SMASHY SMASHY

The passion for destruction is a creative passion, too! —Mikhail Bakunin

ACROSS

1 ___ card (smartphone insert)
4 Astrological boundary
8 Genie's grants
14 Laudatory verse
15 Tennis stadium eponym
16 Drawstring tips
17 Practice the KonMari method before sabotaging feedlots?
19 Single-file
20 Shoreline phenomena
21 City known for the first public park
23 Ancient theatres
24 Springtime story of trashing real estate?
28 Acknowledged (to)
30 Before, in verse
31 Came in first
32 Pooh's gloomy pal
35 Courts
36 Viking prayer said before pillaging shopping malls?
40 ___ rate (modem speed measure)
41 Ditching, as a tail
42 Morning times: Abbr.
43 Oaxacan uncle
45 Noteworthy 1994 Kevin Smith film
49 Garamond and Bodoni graffiti on a vandalized storefront?
53 Horse trot
54 Shisha device
55 Rani's dress: Var.
56 One of the Virgin Islands
59 Conservative charged with destroying property?
61 Big star on the small screen
62 Tag sale caveat
63 ___ Tomé
64 Part of OSHA
65 Split
66 Spike TV's previous name

DOWN

1 Indulgent
2 Repetitive assent
3 Combined, in cards
4 Bengal and Burmese
5 Manipulate, say
6 Food brand for 4-Down
7 Dinero in the Dominican Republic
8 Certain server
9 Pay no attention to
10 Bias in an op-ed
11 2013 Spike Jonze film about AI
12 DDE's command in WWII
13 Direction from Chicago to Memphis: Abbr.
18 Like some jobs
22 Prepares tea
24 Breyer's competitor
25 Like one who's off base?
26 Weaver's machine
27 Some dashes
29 Brainwave test: Abbr.
33 "What's that?!?"
34 Site of the 2014 World Cup, briefly
35 Economic indicator of privilege
36 Hobbled
37 Remove from office
38 Insta posts
39 Where Baldwin takes on Trump
40 Tavern
43 "Hold the jalapeños!"
44 Counterfactual phrase
46 Least numerous
47 Macaulay Culkin's brother
48 Squash, as an insect
50 New England island name
51 Pertaining to birth
52 The ones over there
55 Part of CBS
56 They cross aves.
57 New Deal electrification prog.
58 Peanut butter brand
60 Shedding workers, in short order

ANARCHO-SYNDICALISM

ACROSS

1 Rock musician honored with a statue in Prague
6 Averred
12 Grub
16 Olympic weapons
17 North American peak
18 Kondabolu of comedy
19 DIY politics
21 Deeply impressed
22 Singer who notably covered "Lady Marmalade"
23 Book excerpt
25 Signs up for
28 Organizational principle
31 Signal to perform
32 Legislator's assistant
33 Layers of ore
34 Anti-capitalist activity
40 Care for others
41 ___ Locks (Huron-Superior link)
42 Opening of "The Banana Boat Song"
46 Wet or dry cocktail
47 Dismissively respond
49 Greek portico
50 Spanish 61-Across
52 Playgrounds for pooches
53 Ultimate mass action
55 Peter of NPR's *Wait Wait ... Don't Tell Me!*
59 Resort city San ___
60 Panhandle
61 Workers' organization
64 Stand-up star Tig
67 Put at ease
68 Fett in the *Star Wars* universe
69 Lacking width or depth
70 Noted syndicalist (1873-1958)
77 Bash of CNN
78 Red Sea peninsula
79 Getting by (out)
80 Those: Sp.
81 Alpine echoes
82 Aligns apps across devices

DOWN

1 #26 in British English
2 Prefix pertaining to bees
3 Apiece
4 Dyed marshmallow treats
5 PC data format
6 Place for Pierre: Abbr.
7 Old slang for an investigator
8 Kitchen pest
9 Mai ___
10 Marry in secret
11 Currency in Kuwait
12 Virginal
13 Pacific state
14 Pacific Coast state
15 Enlarges, as a highway
20 Spike TV, formerly
24 Put some money aside
25 ___ Razor
26 Tug upon
27 ___ alla Scala (Milan opera house)
28 Unyielding
29 URL end for Ohio Univ.
30 Ohio Univ. handouts?
32 Start to a Twitter handle
35 Maracaibo's equivalent to mlle.
36 ___ generis (unique)
37 From that time
38 Leave the band
39 Pines (for)
42 Costly
43 Above, in Spanish
44 One who goes on and on
45 New York county or lake
48 Competent, facetiously
51 Hatcher of *Desperate Housewives*
52 Pulitzer Prize-winning Kendrick Lamar album
53 Series for Jane Lynch
54 Vintage car inits.
55 Walked purposefully
56 Venues for rock concerts
57 Illinois home of U. S. Grant
58 European sportswear company
62 Sunburn cause
63 ___ psychology
64 "... deserve neither liberty ___ safety" (Franklin)
65 Double-reed winds
66 Less than cultured
68 30-Down for budding writers
71 Stereotypical lover of puns
72 Both David and Victoria Beckham, e.g.
73 ___ Nas X
74 Siblings and such
75 Env. insert
76 Members of the O-line

1	2	3	4	5		6	7	8	9	10	11		12	13	14	15
16						17							18			
19					20								21			
			22							23		24				
25	26	27					28	29	30							
31						32						33				
34			35	36	37					38	39					
40									41				42	43	44	45
46										47		48				
49					50		51		52							
				53				54								
55	56	57	58				59							60		
61					62	63					64	65	66			
67									68							
69					70		71	72	73					74	75	76
77					78							79				
80					81							82				

LEADERLESS RESISTANCE

ACROSS

1 Title character in *The Lion King*
6 Tasteless
10 Minor dent in a fender
14 Amass compulsively
15 "___ Kleine Nachtmusik"
16 Trendy berry
17 Silent vigil
20 Member of a Biblical sect
21 Bread for a panini
22 Hunger strike, essentially
24 ___ Lobos
25 Sit-in
33 Gainsay
34 Pole or Croat
35 Take second, in a way
36 Licenses or passports: Abbr.
37 Difficult position
39 Non-___ (health food label)
40 Mary Trump, notably
42 One in Innsbruck
43 For a circle, it's πr^2
44 Strike action
47 Thurman of films
48 Rug specification
49 Meltdown
54 Venice's marketplace
58 Revolution
60 Widely quoted "author": Abbr.
61 Et ___ (and others)
62 Column style
63 ___ chocolate chip
64 Food that's trucked in?
65 Spot for a tat

DOWN

1 Flat, for example
2 Electrically charged particles
3 Dallas team, for short
4 In a concise manner
5 Word in a Hebrew blessing
6 Host of *Full Frontal*
7 Merc cousin
8 Opposed to
9 Miami newspaper
10 Quantitative research need
11 Portrayer of Tutuola on *Law & Order: SVU*
12 19th-century cartoonist
13 Bhagavad ___
18 Not as much as
19 Double reed player
23 Nahuatl-speaking people
25 Singer Menzel
26 Like 13-Down
27 Atlas miniature
28 Rudimentary
29 Bring into balance
30 *Empire* co-author
31 Walk-on role
32 Online finance company
37 Jazzman Woody
38 Have high hopes
41 Was unable to
43 Consumed mass quantities
45 Barks in another's direction
46 Piano-playing Keys
49 Do last-minute prep for an exam
50 Westin competitor
51 Grammy-winning Kings of ___
52 Toni Morrison's second novel
53 Idle guy?
55 Active URL
56 Drudgery
57 Glen Hansard musical
59 ___ Grande

VISION FOR BLACK LIVES

m4bl.org

ACROSS

1 Cannabis fiber
5 Opera by Puccini
10 Downsides
14 Digging up dirt, politically
15 Denzel Washington received one for *Glory*
16 Be next to
17 Florida Marlins uniform color
18 ___D. (druggist's degree)
19 Authorization to see your FBI file: Abbr.
20 Invest in education, . . . (part of OHS)
23 Some germ cells
24 Skye of Hollywood
25 Economic justice through . . . (aim of some tax plans)
32 EPA stat
33 Solange, to Beyoncé
34 Serena Williams' game
36 Student
39 Type of gift
41 Early blues style
42 Rows between rows
44 Problematic character on *The Simpsons*
46 Possible destination from LGA
47 Real democracy and . . . (goal for some parties)
51 ___ Bator
52 Trojans of the Pac-12
53 Community control of institutions, . . . (acts of government)
61 "Didn't see you there . . ."
62 Singer whose "1, 2 Step" was a hit
63 Edit menu function
64 Sequel to Melville's *Typee*
65 White-plumed heron
66 Scrolling key
67 Habitually harmful
68 WWI battle site
69 Nays partner

DOWN

1 Planet in *The Empire Strikes Back*
2 Olympic event
3 Movie rating grp.
4 Hoi ___
5 Formal wear in 1930s films
6 Govt. factory inspectors
7 Image-making operation
8 Notable woman of rap
9 Signal for an embrace
10 Espresso's kick
11 High woodwind
12 *La ___ étoilée* (van Gogh painting)
13 Puppy school command
21 DVD output devices
22 Contributed to the pot
25 ___ Nui
26 Provide with gear
27 Maniac prefix
28 Contrive a result
29 Hall of Fame musician Hayes
30 Set to simmer
31 Saltpeter, in England
35 ___ City (Baghdad district)
37 Magician's art
38 Netflix dystopian drama
40 Dean's list qualifying stat
43 Positions on political issues
45 Wail
48 Duke Ellington's "Mood ___"
49 Pressure measure: Abbr.
50 Sit-in, say
53 Weaver's apparatus
54 Expressive sigh found in Paul Lawrence Dunbar's "Sympathy"
55 "Stop!"
56 Chicken ___ (Italian dish, for short)
57 Utah town
58 *Picnic* playwright
59 Scandinavian epic
60 Boys in the family

GENDER TROUBLE

Unscramble some words for a gender "reveal"

ACROSS

1 Board book basics
5 Analog way to pay
9 Terra ___
14 Political coalition
15 Mont Blanc, par exemple
16 "… partridge in ___ tree"
17 Musician and activist Song (Rising Appalachia)
18 Gull relative
19 Museum piece
20 What you hear as cabbies wait on Christmas Eve? (*Change one's orientation.*)
23 Apple computer
24 Cold desert
25 Hyphenated name for a fruit drink
28 Bakery treat
32 Mock Spanish disapproval used in Grumpy Cat memes
34 Atomic number of H
35 Brief, perhaps self-contradictory, disclaimer
37 Sound of laughter
38 Sneezing or gagging, for example? (*There is more than one way to be.*)
43 Regulation in the Federal Register
44 Kobe's antagonistic teammate
45 Due successor?
46 Got married, performatively
50 Trod through melted snow
52 Cinematic street of nightmares?
53 Rather glum
55 English class, for short
56 Prepare a book of haiku? (*Alter one's sense of self.*)
62 Mobile camera
64 ___ B'rith
65 Take a refresher course, say
66 Adulterate
67 "___ avocado a fruit?"
68 Theta follower
69 Sandwich cookies coming in 25 varieties
70 Mao's immediate successor
71 Russian monarch

DOWN

1 In a skillful manner
2 Comme le ciel
3 Pennsylvania product
4 Ponzi follower
5 Underground burial site
6 Game show host Trebek (who is missed by many)
7 Bit of parsley
8 Muppet creator Jim
9 "Bodak Yellow" singer
10 Volkswagen rival
11 Modern medium for a doctor
12 ___ chi ch'uan
13 Plot's path
21 Short putt
22 Like the novelist Chimamandu Ngozi Adichie
26 Location revealing phrase
27 Urged, in a flattering manner
28 Boorish
29 Like the totals on a W-2
30 South Florida dessert
31 Often mispronounced soup
33 Letters on vintage TVs
36 Places for some RNs
39 Iraq War concern: Abbr.
40 UK system founded by Aneurin Bevan
41 Bouncing back, say
42 Give gear to
47 Mad had its "usual gang" of them
48 URL component
49 Beaten in an auction
51 Exasperated parent's shout
54 Dental hygienist's command
57 1962 Bond film
58 Tandoor bread
59 Cupid analogue
60 Physics prefix
61 Practice in a ring
62 Surf music subject: Abbr.
63 Paddle for a pontoon

ACROSS

1 "___ Lisa" (Lil Wayne song)
5 Straightaway: Abbr.
9 Centers of solar systems
13 Requests something (of)
17 Part of QED
18 Guam, e.g.
19 In ___ (aligned)
20 2002 in a movie copyright
21 Ignite
23 Superior sprinter
25 Activities for 87-Across
27 Manuel II of Portugal, e.g.
28 Job ad initials
29 Superlative suffix
30 Focus for 87-Across
37 Gibbon, say
40 Musical based on *La Bohème*
41 Democratic selection process
42 ___ access
43 Alpine trill
45 Birth MDs
46 Oenophile's asset
48 Pesters
50 Policy ___
51 Relief provided by 87-Across
53 Cholesterol medication
55 Policy position
56 Whitney Houston label
60 Streaming music app
64 Ultimate aim for 87-Across
67 Actors in a film
70 Ripped
71 Transports in a Tiananmen Square photo
72 Car buyer's concern, briefly
73 Signs of muscle strain
75 Suit and ___
76 Tolkien beast
77 Use a teakettle
78 Author of *Immediatism*
79 Concern for 87-Across
84 Oom follower
85 Agy. serving entrepreneurs
86 26-Down for Rudolf Rocker
87 Organization refounded by Stuart Christie and Albert Meltzer
97 Part of a 3-2 count
98 Accuses the President of crimes
99 Doppelgänger
100 Rich soil
101 Ride up the slope
102 Colloquial negative
103 Mechanized weapon used on Hoth
104 Theater seating area
105 Puppy noises
106 The haves and the have-___

DOWN

1 Disarray
2 Popular ice cream add-in
3 MLB league
4 Initially
5 *Take the ___* (Strayhorn composition)
6 Fortune teller
7 Intro to painting, say
8 Took part in a demo
9 Kitchen array
10 Stellar bear
11 Chomsky (of course)
12 Fox in *Dora the Explorer*
13 Sphere of influence
14 Industrial haze
15 Ceramicist's need
16 Takes a chair
22 Prefix with -logical
24 ___ woman
26 "Hey, ___ there!" (paradigm case of interpellation)
30 Senior moments?
31 Provide a counterargument
32 Photo sharing app, for short
33 Queen in Disney's *Frozen*
34 Indian flatbread
35 Surveyor's map
36 Olympic gymnast Korbut
37 Dust-up
38 Authorial metonymy
39 Tundra denizen
44 Accept responsibility for
46 Diplomatic virtue
47 Unangam Tunuu speaker
49 Hunt in a stealthy manner
52 ___ HERE (labor union)
54 Philosopher and novelist Murdoch
57 Host of NPR's *Weekend Edition Saturday*
58 Type of sentence
59 It's formed by rays emanating from a vertex
61 Punishment associated with grounding
62 Ontario lake
63 IMHO, essentially
64 Quality of a Bartók composition
65 Milhouse's friend
66 How some programs are delivered
67 Zin alternative
68 Bandage brand
69 Like a wallflower
74 Noisy kiss
77 ___ chicken (grilling option)
80 "Damn it!"
81 Recede
82 Glacial ridges
83 Soc. Sec. tax
84 Cursive alternative
87 Terrier in *The Thin Man*
88 Cereal box abbr.
89 Operatic number
90 "___, Sing America" (Langston Hughes poem)
91 Giveaways
92 Prefix with -dextrous
93 Machine to treat apnea: Abbr.
94 Home to Kasich and Kucinich
95 Email folder label
96 Concordes, for example

WITH THE WOBBLIES

ACROSS

1 "Wicked" woman
6 Any member of the group noted for "Love Train"
10 Campbell of *Scream* fame
14 *Swan Lake* role
15 Pasta sauce brand
16 Gulf state
17 Fasten again, as fabric
18 Apologetic words
20 One big union (sports)
22 One not yet Wed.
23 H, in Greek
24 Hither partner
25 Like some duties in Confucianism
27 Hollywood's Laura or Bruce
29 Macro key
32 Treads the boards
33 Nay's opposite
35 Peekaboo follower
38 One big union (music)
40 Word before Four
41 Land-grant inst. in Ft. Collins
42 Town, informally
43 Ibiza, por ejemplo
45 Kropotkin antagonist
49 Stopped by a diner
52 Popular citation style: Abbr.
54 Cry partner
55 Long or Vardalos of movies
56 One big union (relationships)
60 Request for an explanation
62 It's attached to the left ventricle
63 The Hartford logo
64 Swiss river
65 A singular pronoun
66 Knuckleballer Wilhelm
67 Instant oatmeal instruction
68 Let up

DOWN

1 Artfully obtained a confession (out of)
2 Conceive
3 Container by a register
4 Muse of history
5 TV's Buck
6 Problematic concept analyzed by Edward Said
7 Hooded resident of Tatooine
8 King defeated by Samuel
9 ___ Islam (formerly Cat Stevens)
10 "___ any drop to drink" (Coleridge)
11 <3
12 Pacific nation
13 Partner and patron of Marx
19 Wu ___ (Daoist principle)
21 Neighborhood, say
26 Sun bathe
28 Oscar-winning actress Lupita
30 Serious splits
31 2020 college football champs
34 Remarkably, the bald eagle is one
36 Ford SUV model
37 Component of glaciers in die Alpen
38 Eroded
39 Classical start to the 7th century
40 Opened, as a watermelon
42 Send packing, in a way
44 Legal counsel
46 Areas around many county towns
47 Close relative, familiarly
48 Esteem
50 Thurman of *Pulp Fiction*
51 Brief farewells
53 "It's ___! See you then!"
57 Take care of a fly
58 Traditional Indian garment
59 Qatari capital
61 Driver's license abbr.

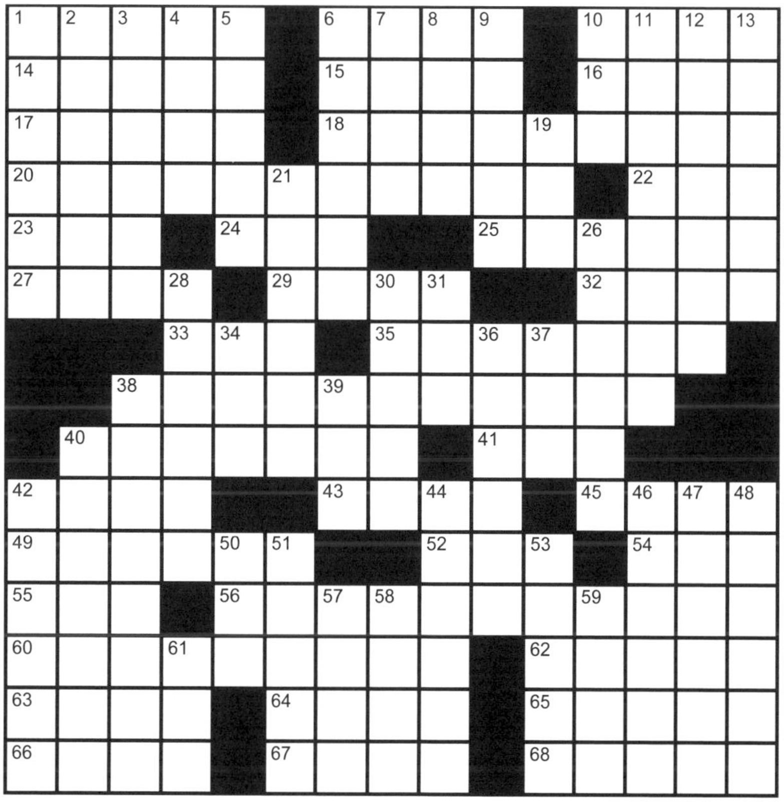
1 2 3 4 5 6 7 8 9 10 11 12 13
14 15 16
17 18 19
20 21 22
23 24 25 26
27 28 29 30 31 32
33 34 35 36 37
38 39
40 41
42 43 44 45 46 47 48
49 50 51 52 53 54
55 56 57 58 59
60 61 62
63 64 65
66 67 68

FREE WOMEN / *MUJERES LIBRES*

ACROSS

1 Stirnerite school of thought
7 Site of the Burj Khalifa
12 OPEC units
16 Producer of Lts.
19 Actor who played Lugosi in *Ed Wood*
20 Getty played by Christopher Plummer
21 Dynamic prefix?
22 Italy's counterpart to the BBC
23 Anarchist, educator, and Communard (1830-1905)
25 Throwing a tantrum, say
27 As well
28 Bush 43 re Bush 41
29 Anarcho-communist author of *The Politics of Individualism*
31 Like some teas
34 DC major leaguer
35 ___ Tages (one day): Ger.
36 American anarchist and free-thinker (1866-1912)
43 Troy story
44 In bed no longer
45 "___ Beso" (1962 Paul Anka hit)
46 Moo goo ___ pan
49 Activist and author of *Anarchism and Its Aspirations*
54 Hearty reds
57 Long, long time
58 Hautbois
59 Verbal pauses
61 Act like a ghost
62 Actor Pickens in *Blazing Saddles*
63 Not altogether there
66 OutKast, for one
67 Poet and co-founder of *Mujeres Libres* (1895-1970)
72 Cupid's comrade
73 Hose material
74 Rim or brim
75 *This Week* network
76 Home of the NCAA's Nittany Lions
77 Notable Joni Mitchell album
78 Musical Amos
82 See 89-Across
84 Political theorist and biographer of 105-Across
89 With 82-Across, Alphonse Mucha's genre
90 Written with five sharps
92 Hand needed to open
93 Protestant ___
94 Spanish anarchist co-founder of *Mujeres Libres* (1901-1994)
100 "Feed me," from a French feline
103 Yes, in Yokohama
104 Rumor debunking site
105 Anarchist author of *Living My Life* (1869-1940)
109 Airport personnel: Abbr.
110 ___ walks
114 Fib that's no big deal
115 Author of *Socialism, Anarchism, and Feminism*
119 High
120 Mama's mama
121 New Orleans neighborhood
122 Feed another's habit
123 Intelligence operative
124 Never have I ___ (party game)
125 Pert
126 Speak against

DOWN

1 Jazz great Fitzgerald
2 Wilde's *The Ballad of Reading ___*
3 Responsibility
4 Singular prefix
5 ___ in "Saskatchewan"
6 Breakfast fare in Berne
7 Spirit mentioned in the Quran
8 Lines to scan: Abbr.
9 Part of Scrooge's catchphrase
10 *The Clan of the Cave Bear* author
11 Aches and pains
12 Brew with a triangle logo
13 Trial runs for apps
14 Hubbard who founded Scientology
15 Serious
16 Rigel's constellation
17 "___ talk?" (loaded question)
18 Endorses a check
24 Othello, for example
26 ___-dieu (prayer site)
30 Sch. in Chapel Hill
31 Suffragist Elizabeth ___ Stanton
32 Ouzo flavoring
33 In case something worse happens
36 Digital media company
37 Hodgepodge
38 Scottish audio electronics brand
39 Tiny bits
40 Expected to come
41 ___Pen (injector for allergic reactions)
42 Thee successor
46 Sagrada Familia architect
47 Abrogate
48 Analogy phrase
50 Grinder
51 Hieroglyphic bird
52 Family in *Death of a Salesman*
53 "Soup to ___" (comic strip)
55 Alternative to Like or Comment
56 ___ Crunch
60 "Song of ___" (Whitman poem)
62 Strainer
63 LXV * V
64 Palindromic gotcha
65 Top rating, often
66 Federer of pro tennis
67 Source of value for Marx
68 Neither censored nor edited
69 Video surveillance: Abbr.
70 Stooge's laugh
71 In unison, musically
72 Actress Delany of *China Beach*
76 Joke's payoff
77 *Don Juan* author
78 Disapproves, audibly
79 Workplace monitor: Abbr.
80 ___ rage
81 An Andean empire
83 It surrounds us
85 Dr. Zaius of sci-fi fame
86 Some grad. students
87 Sounds from a wino in the comics
88 Storm and Tracker
91 Do me a favor ...
94 Castle defense
95 Levy of *Schitt's Creek*
96 Not all that bright
97 ___ Crüe

98 Altar location

99 Drab fowl with an iridescent mate

100 Cat litter sounds

101 Understood, slangily

102 Cordial relations

106 Royal name in Norway

107 Puts on a performance

108 Prefecture neighboring Kyoto

110 Kill on open mic night

111 Ones Fox hosts seek to own

112 Public Ivy in SoCal

113 Singular pronoun

116 ___ *publica* (commonwealth)

117 Meditative expressions

118 Messenger ___

A MEDITATION ON THE STATE

ACROSS

1 Hosiery shade
6 Each
10 River giant
15 ___ d'état
19 Or else, in music
20 Field rodent
21 Burning charcoal
22 Certain Rwandan
23 Bakunin's observation on the state, part 1
27 Frolic in the ocean
28 PBS science series
29 Styling gels
30 "The ___ of the moral universe . . ."
31 Big to-do
33 Top rating, sometimes
34 Charged particles
35 Started anew
38 Exercise junkie
40 Hot group for Korean teens
41 Piglet nursers
45 Piglet snout
47 Next to
49 Resound, like a protest chant
50 . . . part 2
53 . . . part 3
57 Light brown
58 Orange-yellow color
60 Janelle of *Moonlight*
61 ___ chanty
62 When the witches last appear in *Macbeth*
64 Making blades sharp
67 ___-Manuel Miranda
68 Last traces
70 . . . part 4
71 Author of "Anarchic Thoughts on Anarchism"
76 Feel some regret

77 World Series perfect-game pitcher
79 "___ Easy" (Buddy Holly tune)
80 Prereq for a PhD student
83 Short nails
86 Decorative items
88 Promises not to squeal: Abbr.
89 . . . part 5
93 . . . part 6
95 Revealing glow
96 Enduring
97 Chinese currency
98 Abound (with)
99 Target in an alley
101 Wenger of Premier League fame
103 Italian scooter
107 Sound of complaint
109 "Cathy" exclamation
110 Highway
112 Magic, on a sports ticker
113 Subsaharan grassland
116 Place for a goatee
118 Bangle
121 . . . part 7
124 Counselor role in "Star Trek: The Next Generation"
125 Garlicky sauce
126 Nice nothing
127 Like some music or crosswords
128 Rock music's Suzanne
129 Attack
130 Anarchist writer Colin
131 Prone to talking back

DOWN

1 Trailer hitch
2 On land, to a sailor
3 Garage sale purchase
4 Like an air freshener, say

5 Diner offering
6 C-worthy
7 High shot
8 "Bravo!" in Baja California
9 Lowly worker
10 Gaul neighbor
11 That is to say . . .
12 Kegler's grp.
13 Participants in direct action don't seek one
14 Cookie-based cereal
15 Knights' lair
16 Yeses in Ypres
17 ___ *Reader* (onetime hip magazine)
18 Dogs with flat muzzles
24 Embrace
25 Soapmaking ingredient
26 Certain hairstyle
32 Sleep-inducing med
36 Sense
37 Court-filing pseudonym
39 Legal do-over
40 O'Rourke of Texas
42 Folksinger Phil
43 Water slide sound
44 Bean plant
46 ___-cone (icy treat)
48 Psych. reference
50 "The ___" (nickname in '50s TV)
51 Behold, to Claudius
52 Liberal follower?
53 "___ a good dog?!?"
54 Amherst, relative to Boston
55 Forgettable 2012 presidential candidate
56 *How to Be an Anti-Racist* author
59 Marin of comedy fame
63 Key Machiavellian concept
65 Gun rights grp.

66 Room pets
69 Brief side at a taqueria
71 Shakespearean monarch
72 Time for a meeting or a meal
73 IRS home
74 Actor Morales
75 *The Joy of Painting* host
78 Planting apparatus
80 Bothersome insect
81 Rascal
82 French 101 verb
84 R&B's Chaka ___
85 Droop
87 Alma mater of Dick Gregory: Abbr.
90 Puppy class
91 Cobbler stone?
92 Canine hybrid
94 Top choice, briefly
97 Late December, say
99 Bamboo consumers
100 One way for the game to conclude
102 "whether 'tis ___ in the mind . . ."
104 Cylinders and cubes
105 Summary
106 Shortcut tool
108 Premier prime
109 Northeast Corridor transport
111 ___ *Kapital*
113 Onetime vehicle for Short and Levy
114 Alpine river
115 YouTube series, maybe
117 Neighbor of Swe.
119 Several related CBS dramas
120 Sicilian volcano
122 Spicy, as a dish
123 Actress Zadora

SONGS OF THE WILD

WILD TO THE END

ACROSS

1 What the goat says
4 Principle of nonviolence
10 Chocolate dogs
14 Music registry service: Abbr.
19 Surprised interjections
20 Flaw
21 Un océano
22 ___ for time
23 Notable Spike Lee joint (The Troggs 1965)
26 Shout out, colloquially
27 Verdi's "La donna è mobile"
28 "I ___ all to . . ." (words of gratitude)
29 Core strategy
31 Monumental (Paul McCartney 1971 or Talking Heads 1986)
36 Like a grizzly
37 First step in a proof
38 Mao's successor
40 Part of MIT: Abbr.
41 Animosities
44 Islamic tradition
48 Like wine in vats
50 Somewhat
51 Group Beyoncé left behind (Iggy Pop 1986, Enya 2001, or Kenny Chesney 2014)
54 Kid who's a handful
57 São ___
59 Spanish royal
60 Pub potables
61 The "watercourse way" per Alan Watts
62 Woman in Wiesbaden
63 Like foggy days
64 Santa ___ (California winds)
65 Singer Erykah
66 "Be quiet!"
67 Parts of some bldgs.
68 Pithy summary: Abbr.
69 Wallflower, say
70 Enthusiastic
71 Afrobeat pioneer Kuti
72 Smallest
73 Menu heading
74 Sun. follower
75 Otherwise
76 Beat poet Gregory
77 Authority
79 Experienced one
80 Ambience in sensory deprivation tank (Moby 2018)
84 Managed care grp.
85 US steel producer
87 Subject of Herman & Chomsky's *Manufacturing Consent*
88 Stimulated
90 Paradise
92 Cabo da ___ (Portuguese point)
94 "Cool!"
95 Minnesota iron ore range
97 "Wait a second!" (The Rolling Stones 1970)
105 Pre-CD recording medium
107 "Alley Oop" character
108 Opportunity to show off, musically
109 Christensen of TV's *Parenthood*
110 Florida attraction (Cat Stevens 1970)
115 Duck down
116 Virginie, par exemple
117 "I'm stumped."
118 Lapsong Souchong, e.g.
119 Garden catalog offering
120 In ___ (actually)
121 Cathedral sounds
122 Response: Abbr.

DOWN

1 Most frequent
2 Now, in Nicaragua
3 Moving about
4 Drink suffix
5 Gendered possessive
6 "___ had only . . ." (rueful words)
7 Large unit of resistance
8 Unstressed vowel sound
9 "BBC News ___"
10 Actress Christine of *Swing Shift*
11 Form 1040 fig.
12 Elastic cord
13 *Game of Thrones*, say
14 Author of *The Beatles from A to Zed*
15 Visits
16 Leaving the party, say (Van Morrison 1971)
17 Arbus and Antliff
18 Type of orbiter
24 "Horrible" comic character
25 Up to, commercially
30 Non-magical types
32 Deleted
33 Take the train
34 Pitch
35 Savings saver? (Abbr.)
39 Expressions at your fingertips?
41 With it
42 Out of kindness
43 Nagging problem (Lou Reed 1972 or Mötley Crüe 1987)
44 Afternoon nap
45 Liters and meters
46 The "city so nice they named it twice" (Abbr.)
47 Electronic surveillance org.
49 Some badges
52 Top level of Minor League Baseball
53 Practical experience
55 Didn't experience delays
56 Some ounces of wine
58 Put down
63 Conductor's honorific
64 Iditarod locale
65 Portend
66 Drag show flair
68 Juno Award-winning musician Clark
69 Offer, as a long-term rental
71 Put the pedal to the metal
72 Washer contents
75 And so forth, briefly
76 Notes between B and F
78 Layer of a lawn
81 Amused initialism
82 Still life subject
83 Pre-revolutionary leader of Iran
86 Like some intrusive questions
89 Trunk
90 Does intros and segues
91 Honey
93 Buys a term paper, say
94 Subtlety
96 Carries, as a burden
98 Tony winner Lenya
99 Pentagon agy.

100 Snatching sound on "The Simpsons"

101 Cohort of Kent and Lane

102 Somewhat

103 ___ Ochoa, first Latina in space

104 Carbondated drinks

106 Cutesy

111 Start for Vegas?

112 Architectural annex

113 Brynner of the movies

114 Film director Craven

ABOLITIONIST SLOGANS

ACROSS

1 Author of *The Rebel*
6 Big name in eyewear
12 Jamaican music genre
15 Taken aback
16 Shoreline hazard
17 Tolkein creature
18 Defund the ___! Come as you are!
20 Really exciting
21 Symphony dedicated to heroism
22 Insult
23 Overturn ___! Who needs it anyway?
30 Je t'___
31 Small point to obsess about
32 San Francisco happenings, once
33 Ruins, as a parade
35 Frankie of the Four Seasons
37 1960's Russian chess champion
38 Forerunner to Python?
39 Sources of legal precedent
41 End ___! Don't buy "Risk"!
46 Large amount, idiomatically
47 Any hit by 35-Across
49 Yo te ___
52 Sandwich chain with "the meats"
53 Welsh football side
55 Onesie protector
57 ___ poetica
58 Numeric guesses: Abbr.
59 A toxic waste dump is a ___. Clean it now!
63 Fla. neighbor
64 Insects noted for pincers
65 "The Greatest"
66 Ban the ___! RIP OED!
73 Prefix to place?
74 Perennial
75 *Goosebumps* author
76 Prattle
77 Musical prodigy of the 18th century
78 *CBS This Morning* competitor

DOWN

1 Part of a rhyming latte order
2 Turkish title
3 Some advanced degrees: Abbr.
4 Show to a seat, shortly
5 Elevator pitch
6 Reformation-era fighting word
7 Steve's role on *Boardwalk Empire*
8 Dwight's two-time opponent
9 Hitter's stat
10 Secreted resin
11 Poetic "before"
12 Ask for something
13 *Bhagavad Gita* figure
14 Comedian's set
16 Isolate, as with a winter cabin
19 University town in Maine
22 Dr. of rap
23 Message from a Manx: Var.
24 Acid found in protein
25 Nissan make
26 Daytime TV's DeGeneres
27 Missouri city near the Ozarks
28 Pilot
29 Noted fashion monogram
30 Sleeve insert
34 Professorial handouts
35 "Let's go!" in Nuevo Laredo
36 Snarky "Not likely . . ."
39 Commander of 1950s serials
40 Wonka portrayer
42 Style of column
43 Yabba ___ Doo! (toon catch-phrase)
44 Pindar, for one
45 Sweet, once
48 Majority of fluff
49 Paragon of easiness
50 Jackson of gospel fame
51 Washington Monument, e.g.
53 Royal headgear
54 Savory jelly
56 Singing Sumac
57 Civil disobedience outcome, perhaps
60 *Futurama* character
61 Kitchen tool
62 Disgorge
65 Non-governmental Schumer
66 Icon for Aries
67 Max Stirner's concern
68 Moroccan city or cap
69 Battle of Seattle target
70 Human- or fact- follower
71 Genetic polymer
72 Largo, for one

SOLUTION: 121, TOP LEFT

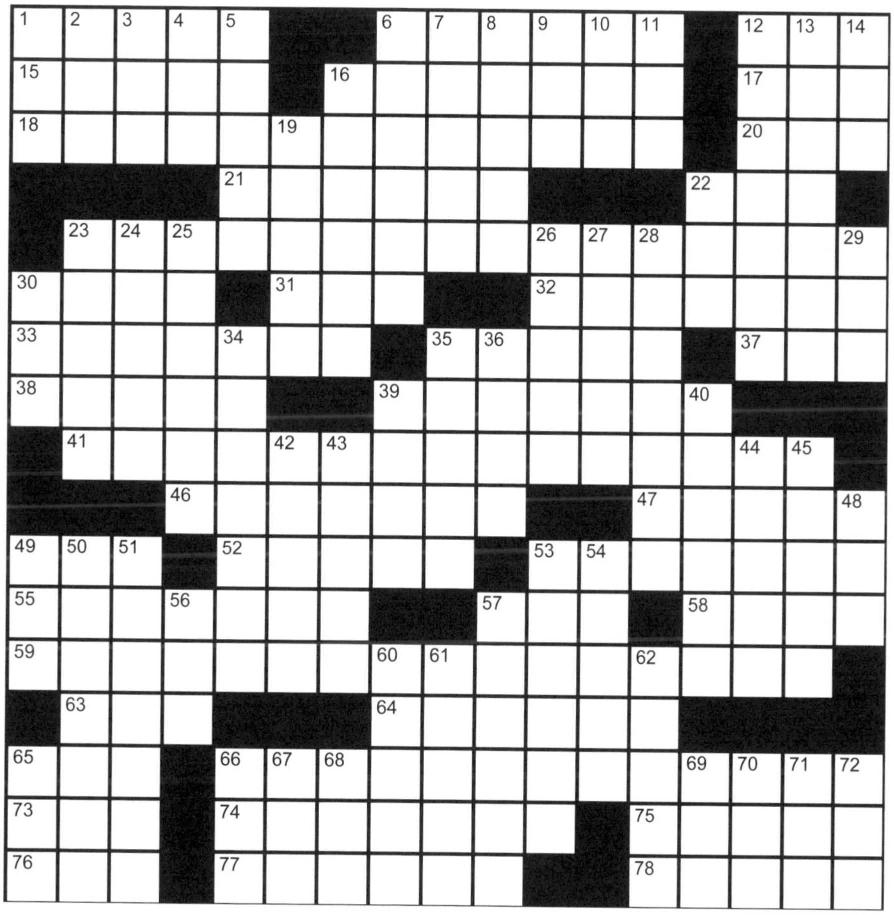

COMPANION PLANTING

PERMACULTURE AND SYMBIOSIS

ACROSS

1 Actor Matthew of *The Boys in the Band*

6 Sandwich counter

10 Author of *The Intelligent Woman's Guide to Socialism and Capitalism*

14 Largest city in Yemen

15 Horse halter?

16 "El Cóndor ___" (Simon and Garfunkel song)

17 Biscuits served with strawberries

19 Lubricates

20 Neighbor of The Bronx

22 Ore-___ (potato product brand)

23 Bless, in a way

24 Branded writer?

30 "Beowulf," for one

31 Tea time offering

32 ___ alai

35 Representative emblem

37 Article in *La Jornada*?

38 Sport for tykes

40 Commit espionage

41 Daisy-like flowers

44 K-pop celebrity

45 Some Kroger or Tesco stores

47 Lover's exclamation

50 Monogram of invention?

51 Signature game for NES

57 Ready for business

58 Something to get at 6-Across

60 Singer-songwriter ___ Del Rey

61 Palindromic time

62 People who finish cupcakes

63 Performs a role

64 Rhinitis-treating docs

65 Clay pigeon shooting

DOWN

1 Blows smoke

2 Honolulu County

3 String between L and Q

4 An anchor wears one

5 Like an adult-ish movie

6 Wee drink

7 ___ mouse!

8 Property encumbrance

9 Fit

10 Precisely correct

11 Part of Hispaniola

12 Lewis' lion

13 Did not exist

18 Studies at the last minute

21 ___ of vipers

24 Some are exotic

25 Per item, informally

26 Feel sorry for

27 Intense

28 Printer's supply

29 Provide with weapons, archaically

32 China's imperial gem

33 Heaps

34 Aches and pains

36 Muriel Bowser, who created Black Lives Matter Plaza in DC

39 Site on a college campus

42 Multicolored gelato

43 Squelched

45 Scavengers on the African continent

46 Synagogue leaders

47 Sicilia, per esempio

48 Rapper also known as Makaveli

49 Exhausted

52 Writer of many zine articles: Abbr.

53 Alfredo Bonanno, *From ___ to Insurrection*

54 Na + and Cl -

55 S-shaped molding

56 Parched

59 D-Day craft

SEEDS BENEATH THE SNOW

THE NEW SOCIETY EMERGING FROM THE SHELL OF THE OLD

ACROSS

1 Chasms
5 Sheep talk
8 Persian Gulf city
12 UPS delivery
15 USC rival
16 Citrus beverage, briefly
17 Biblical paradise
18 Kanga's joey
19 Mister
21 Most destitute
23 Economic system(s)
25 KIND product
26 Notable journalistic podcast
29 Status(es)
34 Maniacal start?
35 Berths for boats
36 Be humbled
40 Hip-hop apparel brand
41 Clam digger
45 Control (not!)
50 "Yes, indeed."
51 Put into a bin
53 Pascal oeuvre
56 Mischievous, as a grin
58 Law that mandates accommodations: Abbr.
59 Social order(s)
64 Place for Putin
68 Approached
69 Mode(s) of distributing power
75 Southern beverage
77 "Another time perhaps."
78 Heavy weight
79 Office supply purchase
80 Meyerhoff, author of *Beyond Education*
81 River Thames food fish
82 To date
83 Sole
84 Mens ___
85 Power unit

DOWN

1 Tex-Mex side
2 Official proceedings
3 Splash sound
4 Reindeer-herding people
5 Marketplaces
6 "___ Fideles"
7 Bacterium dependent on oxygen
8 Star of many Scorsese films
9 Theatres of ancient Greece
10 Elevators?
11 Actress MacDowell of *Multiplicity*
12 Prime minister
13 Daily ___ (political website)
14 Obtained
20 Hit ___ (get along)
22 Loc. for Haifa
24 Reprehensible sort
27 Ages ___
28 Flo Rida song (whose title is repeated in the lyrics)
29 Dating app abbr.
30 Israeli PM between Benjamin and Ariel
31 De cabo a ___ (from top to bottom)
32 Dowdy types
33 Subway system
37 One ___ time
38 Vietnamese New Year
39 Tool for gene editing
41 Pronoun separator
42 Summertime treat in Trier
43 Harlem Globetrotters' founder Saperstein
44 Major reference work: Abbr.
46 ___-de-la-Cite (Notre Dame locale)
47 Word preceding a woman's birth surname
48 "Semi" suffix
49 Bite to eat
52 Motivation question
53 Golfer's standard
54 URL ending for 22-Down
55 Incipient
56 First law of motion concern
57 Annoyed with
60 Notoriety (not in a good way)
61 Shoe width spec.
62 Gilda of SNL fame
63 Spine bearing bump on a cactus
65 Bishopric
66 Initial course, briefly
67 When to have brunch, say
70 Undeniable
71 Big name in old Hollywood
72 Philosophical concern
73 Flavor enhancer
74 Adventurous video game
75 Hog hangout
76 Serious trouble

SOLUTION: 121, BOTTOM LEFT

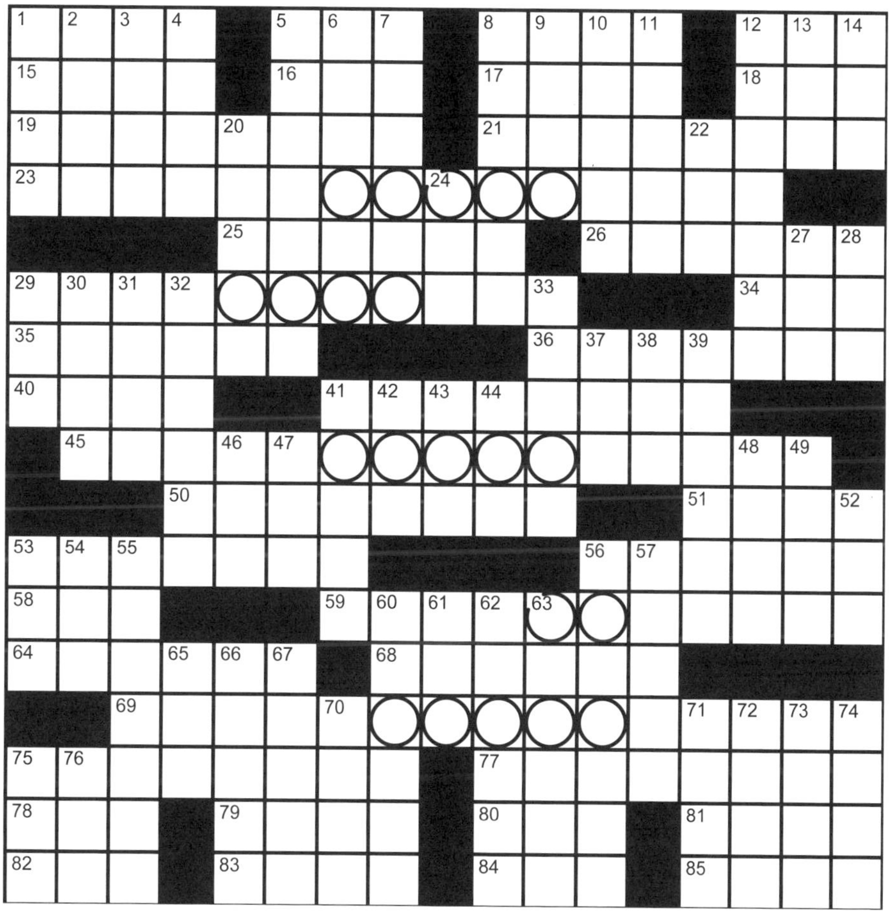

DELEGATES' MEETING

CONNECTIONS AND COMMUNICATION ARE KEY

ACROSS

1 Jet Ski rival

7 Shows discomfort

14 Sheer cotton

16 Cast anew

17 Like an old schoolhouse

18 Observes, furtively

19 Prep for a marathon

20 Some colas, for short

22 Payroll services co.

23 Battle of Normandy town

25 Like the Love Bug's engine

30 "You betcha"

32 Albanian currency

33 Healthy salad green

34 Dating abbr.

37 "Long time, ___"

39 Home for an eaglet

40 Malibu or Monaco

41 Assembly

43 The Kinks' "You Really ___ Me"

44 Keyword in Christian theology

46 Tracking aid

47 They may break ties: Abbr.

48 Vocalizing bird

49 21st in the Greek alphabet

50 Radio frequency abbr.

52 Providing aid

55 Musuem collection

58 Kipling's snake

59 Demolish the interior of a house

61 Christie sleuth Parker ___

63 "Mos def"

67 "Everybody's Talking" singer Harry

69 Does not recall

70 Plutonium discoverer

71 Svelte swimwear

72 Fashion house offerings

DOWN

1 Flue residue

2 Seaside raptors

3 Authorized representative

4 In a foreboding manner

5 *Double Fantasy* performer

6 Body spray target

7 Sometime targets of QBs

8 Get ready to fly home

9 "Don't mind ___" (response to an offer)

10 Irregular kick in soccer

11 Payroll data units: Abbr.

12 ___ psychology

13 VP Kamala Harris, once

15 Community rec center

21 Muffling

24 About 30 mL

26 Volleyball star Gabrielle

27 Key for Bacall

28 *Silas Marner* author

29 Info

31 Dog park detritus

34 Nefarious calls or emails

35 Kobe beef, etc.

36 Swiss unit

38 Offering at some bars

39 On the other hand, briefly

42 Tattoo

45 Subscription box delivery

49 Appeal, as a deity

51 Quickly passes

53 Rowed

54 Target shooter's collection

56 Disinfectant brand

57 Disturb another's sleep, perhaps

60 Evens the score

62 Many Purdue grads

63 Hypotheticals

64 Walk like a wallaby

65 Before, in old verse

66 Total twit

68 Back muscle

SOLUTION: 121, BOTTOM RIGHT

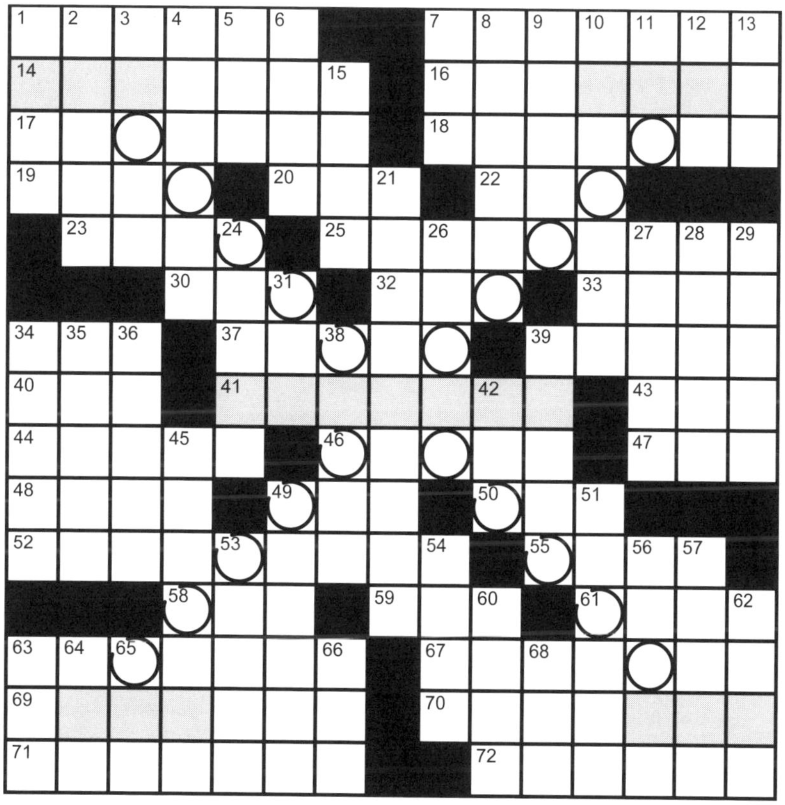

DECLARATION OF A FREETHINKER

WORDS FROM VOLTAIRINE DE CLEYRE

ACROSS

1 ___-ovo vegetarian
6 Brawler's weapons
11 Allan-___ (Robin Hood associate)
16 *The Consolations of Philosophy* author de Botton
17 Observation, part 1
18 Like some fruits
19 Tent type
20 Destroy, as an office record
21 Polo predecessor?
22 Observation, part 2
25 Harried routine
26 Brimless cap
27 NATO region
29 ___ *You My Mother?* (children's book)
30 Some are digital
31 Mend, as a sock
32 Guitar outlet
35 Forest female
37 Certain scofflaw
39 Bellows
42 Get ready, shortly
45 8x10, re a 4x6: Abbr.
46 Observation, part 3
52 More of the same: Abbr.
53 Fly-fishing need
54 The people, to Aristotle
55 Ice-breaking trivia
59 Legal conclusion?
61 Scannable grocery item: Abbr.
62 Binary components
63 Ancestry, metaphorically
66 ___ Dhabi (emirate)
69 Lunch fare, briefly
70 Lorenzini (a.k.a. Collodi), author of *The Adventures of Pinocchio*
71 Slushy, icy drink
75 Observation, part 4
78 Purple, say
79 Tony-winning Webber-Rice musical
80 Certain runner
81 Repeated question in Matthew
82 Observation, part 5
83 Brief bridge bid
84 Male-female binary
85 NIN's Reznor
86 Rapinoe of US soccer fame

DOWN

1 Part of TTYL
2 Smart speaker signifier
3 French royal name
4 ___ del Fuego
5 Small garage
6 Jazzy choreographer
7 ___ *Hollers Let Him Go* (Chester Himes novel)
8 Flash
9 US central bank
10 Humorist David
11 Allow to enter
12 Performance art
13 Ditz
14 Professorial performance
15 Tokugawa capital
23 Way to serve coffee or tea
24 McCormick's machine
28 Purpose of a weekend pass, briefly
30 Streep of movie stardom
31 Investigate, in a way
32 Renowned Dadaist
33 Communication to a calf
34 Generic pet icon
36 Shout in a Greek restaurant
38 Debut hit by Barenaked Ladies
40 Coral constructions
41 Mlle. : Port-au-Prince :: ___ : Santo Domingo
43 Univ. extension?
44 Ones noted for their walk?
47 Canadian author of *In Flanders Fields*
48 Pod member
49 World's second tallest bird
50 Cleanup tool
51 Cancel key
55 Key chain feature
56 Free
57 Smart TV streaming app
58 Hurricane effect
60 Spanish surrealist
64 Host of "Last Week Tonight"
65 "It's better ___ than . . ."
67 Kid's plaintive appeal
68 Like a grizzly
70 Rock in "Fargo"
71 Board game origin
72 Part-owner of The Pequod
73 Delle Donne of the WNBA's Mystics
74 Zac of *Me and Orson Welles*
76 Swag bag
77 Battleship coordinate
78 Gender prefix

#SAYTHEIRNAMES

ACROSS

1 Normandie newborn
5 ___-Manuel Miranda, creator of *Hamilton*
8 Formal ceremony
12 Not all there, metaphorically
15 Cooking fat
16 Actor Fishburne of *The Matrix*
18 Sorta
19 ___, Rest in Power (2/26/12)
21 Yvette, par exemple
22 "What'd ___" (Ray Charles song)
23 Liveliness
24 Grammy-winning Baker
26 Crossword clue staple
28 Noted journalist Wells
30 Promissory notes
32 ___ Ben Adhem
33 Nile dam site
35 ___, Rest in Power (7/13/15)
38 Favor one side
39 Computer core
40 Signal device
41 Has to
42 Other people, perhaps
44 Head honcho: Abbr.
45 ___, Rest in Power (7/6/16)
51 One behaving badly
52 Zippo
53 Polluting energy source
55 Hardly enough
58 Peace, in ancient Rome
59 Frozen waffles brand
60 ___, Rest in Power (5/25/20)
64 Throat infection
65 Poor, as an excuse
66 Tandoori-baked bread
67 Hubbub
69 Mineral state
70 Opportunity to hit
72 When doubled, a kid's train
74 Cain's victim
76 RV connectors?
77 ___, Rest in Power (3/13/20)
82 Lateral ends?
83 Member of a '60s Hall of Fame girl group
84 Car in tow, maybe
85 No longer working: Abbr.
86 Presidential candidate Buttigieg
87 Notable prog rock band
88 ___ Garner, Rest in Power (7/17/14)

DOWN

1 Short order order
2 Canal site
3 Remake, attitudinally
4 Grand brand
5 Carli of women's soccer fame
6 Janis of '60s folk
7 Unfeeling
8 History section
9 Where to find Dylan, often
10 Onetime telecom co.
11 Clinton's Secretary of Transportation
12 Hotel room convenience
13 One of a related set of atoms
14 ___ Arbery, Rest in Power (2/23/20)
17 ___ to go
20 Narcissistic
25 Animated lioness
26 Tree in Trinidad
27 Consume entirely
29 Some poplars
31 Protected activity
34 In opposition to
36 Start of a New Year's Eve song title
37 Rorschach test unit
39 Husband of 86-Across
43 Horror genre's Chaney
44 It sits on First Nations territory
46 Director of *Metropolis*
47 Ctrl-C command
48 "Law and Order" actor
49 Legislator, sometimes
50 See 17-Across
54 Casual gait
55 Noted Suquamish chief
56 Burst into flames
57 Basic geometric calculation
60 I ♥ NY logo designer
61 Accept the truth
62 Second-largest Pakistani city
63 Conductor's cue
64 Japanese noodle
68 Halawy and Medjool
71 Batter measure: Abbr.
73 Solely
75 Bronte character
78 Scoreboard trio
79 Pub potable
80 Nail polish brand
81 Giant bird in *The Arabian Nights*

SOCIAL RELATIONSHIPS

The state is a social relationship; a certain way of people relating to one another. It can be destroyed by creating new social relationships; i.e., by people relating to one another differently. —Gustav Landauer

ACROSS

1 Sports
6 Other, in Ciudad Juarez
10 Grinders
14 Garfield's middle name
15 Club choice
16 Hinge joint
17 Rejects, on Tinder
19 Pavlov, but not his dog
20 Script for a protest?
22 Forage crop
25 Stage whisper
26 Marxist-Leninist, to an anarchist?
30 It put the acid in "acid rock"
31 Map
32 ___ de Gama (explorer and colonialist)
34 Genre for 27-Down
35 Affinity ___ (model for new social relationships)
37 Indian flatbread
41 Trapper of snake-like fish
43 Furry red Muppet
44 Major fast food chain
47 Human chain?
51 Key ___
53 Gary's home
54 Place in a picket line?
58 Title for Judi Dench
59 She might live in Montparnasse
63 Hurdles for aspiring PhDs
64 Dendrite's counterpart
65 Washer companion
66 Coup d'___
67 Dynastic name in China
68 Olivia Colman won it for *The Favourite*

DOWN

1 Existed, once
2 *The Elements of Style* monogram
3 NPR's Shapiro
4 Cabinet number in *Hamilton*
5 Fetid
6 Tin Man's request
7 Star ___
8 Sign of hilarity, in a text
9 Pay to play
10 Comedic vignettes
11 Reveal, in a big way
12 ZZ Top trademarks
13 Intuited
18 Living room piece
21 Baby powder ingredient
22 Tablet array
23 *Dirty Harry* composer Schifrin
24 ___ Blucher (*Young Frankenstein* character)
27 Soap brand
28 Egyptian ___ (spotted cat breed)
29 Egyptian cobra
33 Comedic staples
35 Mop & ___ (floor cleaner)
36 State color?
38 Author of *If I Understood You, Would I Have This Look on My Face?*
39 Religious "right!"
40 Screenwriter Ephron
42 Dark, poetically
44 Something badly assembled
45 Some memes
46 Black Sea region
48 Like some wit
49 Les États-___
50 Enthusiastic assent
52 "Whither thou ___ . . ."
55 Subject for a Monty Python sketch
56 Metered ride
57 Schoenberg's *Moses and ___*
60 Community of five boros
61 Teachers' org.
62 Goof

SOLUTION: 122, BOTTOM LEFT

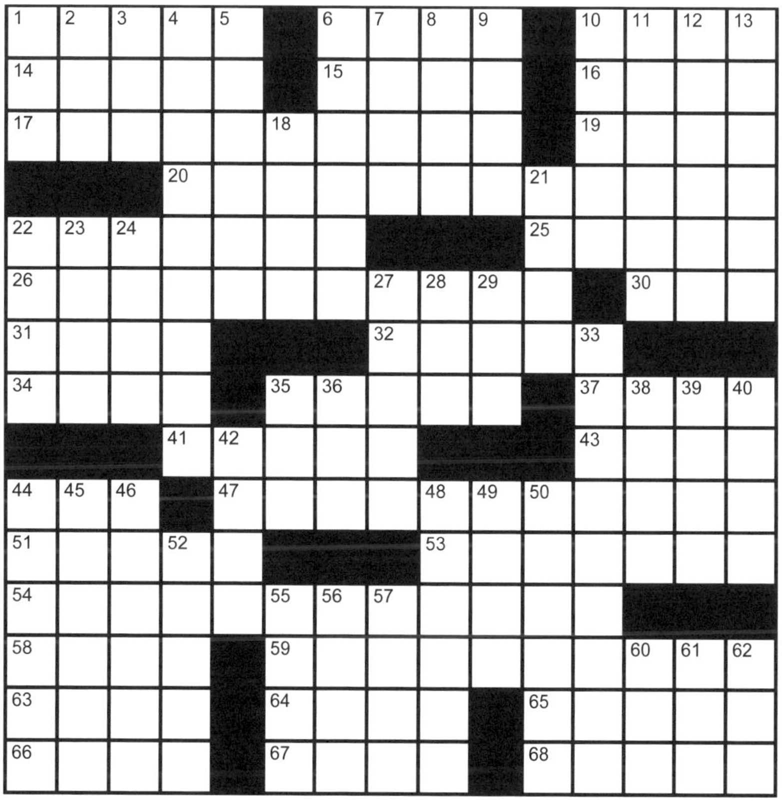

DESTROYING DOMINATION

POWER WORKS IN MYSTERIOUS WAYS (UNRAVEL THE MYSTERY)

ACROSS

1 Fist bump
4 Household automaton
10 Tach figures
14 180° from WNW
15 Deliberately pester
16 Surface dwellers in Wells's *The Time Machine*
17 Freestyle for a good cause? (Men rule!)
19 Canvas shoe brand
20 Model that followed an 8 but not a 9
21 Blues guitarist Clapton
23 Rests atop
24 Single personality flaw? (Barbarism instead of socialism!)
28 Sicilian peak
29 Vocalized sigh of relief
30 Tennis pro Rafael
31 Govt. drafting agency
32 Soil that's more salty than sandy? (Your land is my land!)
35 Green-ish prefix
36 Have a debt
37 Social media share from the Gulf? (This is TERF territory!)
42 AI, for example
45 Coastal hazard
46 Accompagnement de poivre
47 Worker-owned enterprise
48 Snowball to Napoleon, in *Animal Farm*? (The State is everything!)
50 Sound of censure
52 0.5ml per day, say
53 Ristorante dessert
54 Dark shade in poety
56 Stressful junk email? (Free enterprise!)
59 Boxer Riddick
60 Numbers game?
61 "En ___ Casa" (track on *Son de Panamá* by Rubén Blades)
62 Prohibitions
63 China for a good cuppa
64 Rink org.

DOWN

1 Ten percenters?
2 Charcoal grill receptables
3 Farm fowl
4 Massive ungulate
5 Like Cheerios
6 Margaret Atwood novel, ___ *and Crake*
7 Stain or dent
8 Grp. for Cubs and Eagles
9 Colorado ski resort town
10 Play again?
11 Tenor Domingo
12 Calendar abbr.
13 Certain sibling's nickname
18 Santa ___, California
22 Milk-curdling agent
24 Hong Kong entrepreneur Jimmy
25 "Sounds neat."
26 POTUS after Garfield
27 Nightmarish street name
29 Chelsea wing-back Marcos
32 Some mattresses
33 Here, to Henri
34 Pain reactions?
37 Initials of the formal name for mad cow disease
38 Luis von ___, developer of CAPTCHA
39 Square-dance gathering
40 Punk rock's Joey, Dee Dee, Johnny, and Tommy
41 Hit tune from Steely Dan's *Aja*
42 Shut tight
43 Paprika-laden soup
44 Like the best available option
47 Warehouse stuff: Abbr.
49 Caper in a movie
50 Drums from Japan
51 Intact, like some movies
53 Horse trot sound
54 Gradually decline
55 Stereotypical staple of drag
57 Weekly planner abbr.
58 Locale for Ohio Northern University

SOLUTION: 122, BOTTOM RIGHT

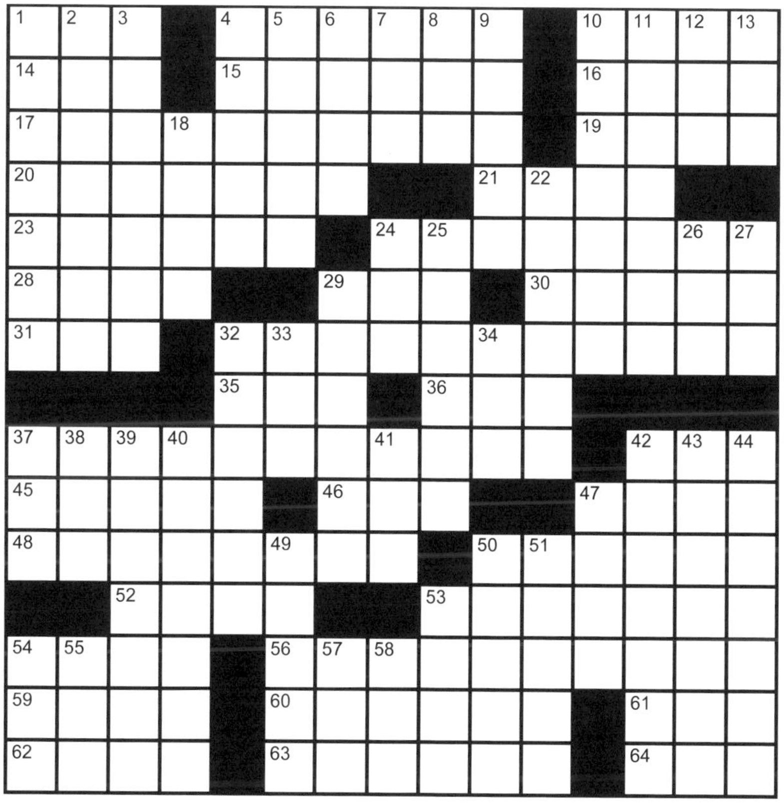

NOISE DEMO

LET'S MAKE SOME NOISE!

ACROSS

1 Informer
5 Foaler
9 Metallic sound
14 European river you might not remember
15 Genesis locale
16 Habitual
17 Imitative bird
18 Melville's captain
19 "Then again . . ."
20 Noises from the kitchen?
23 Alley ___ (classic comic strip)
24 Soothed, as a crying baby
25 Bureaucratic bungle
27 Early vehicle make
29 Chardonnay alternative
33 Noises on the street?
38 Hairnets for the kitchen help
39 Onetime prefix for margarine
40 Lunch or dine
42 Came to earth
43 Sheep
46 Noises on the pitch?
49 Freight train component, at times
51 Bravo in un estadio
52 More achy
54 Standing Rock people
59 Impact sound
62 South American demonstrations (named for 20-Across)
64 Sultan's subject
66 Subject for Democritus
67 Word commonly given a false etymology
68 Like the Tin Man after Dorothy meets him
69 Margarita complement
70 In the before times
71 Brawl
72 List
73 Withdraw gradually (from)

DOWN

1 Natural spirit
2 ___ wish
3 Leases
4 Collision sound
5 Move aimlessly
6 Distracted condition: Abbr.
7 Harvests
8 Like some appellate hearings
9 North side Chicagoan, say
10 Home for some SEC Tigers
11 Self starter?
12 Onetime Apple player
13 Cafeteria serving, at times
21 Dynamic prefix?
22 Slangy refusals
26 Site of the action in *Das Boot*
28 Unity
30 Hang
31 Romeo's parting words
32 Concordes that flew: Abbr.
33 Black marsh bird
34 The A in TAE
35 Control (in)
36 Traffic jam sounds
37 Carpentry tool
41 Nevertheless, briefly
44 Pollution consequence
45 Gilbert known for playing Darlene Conner
47 Bad sign
48 R&B singer with an eponymous 1991 album
50 Manufacturer's bane
53 Solve a lace problem
55 Impact sound
56 Atmospheric layer
57 Puccini opera based on a Sardou play
58 Wan
59 Fireworks sound
60 Friendly fille
61 Hangout for suburban teens
63 Tomato type
65 Born this way (in anniversary announcements)

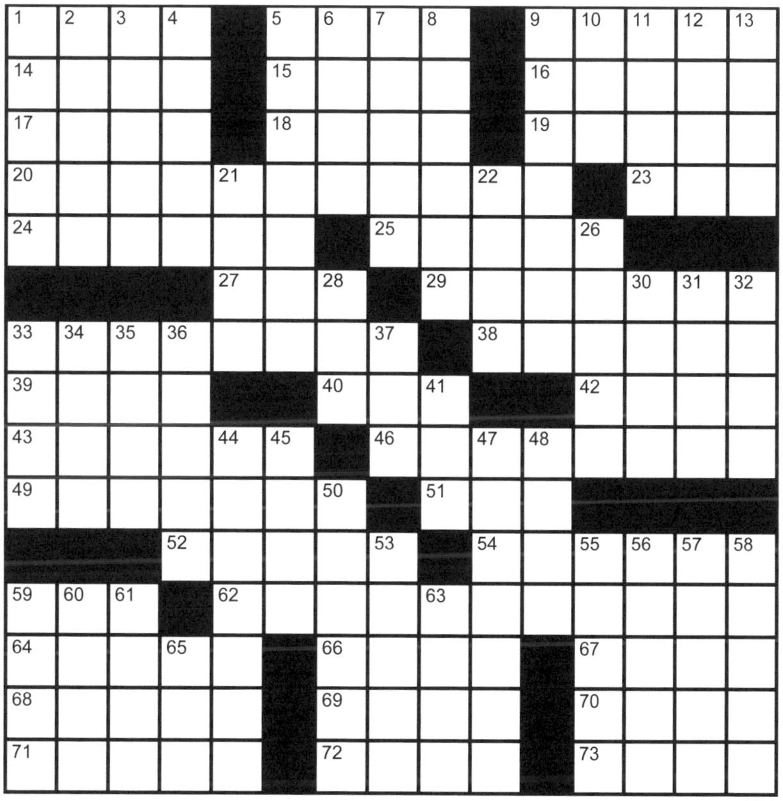

POSTANARCHISM

ACROSS

1 Degree seeker's defense
5 Up a tree
12 Lisa Loeb song used in *Reality Bites*
16 Meh
17 Use a chaise longue
18 Comin' ___ the rye
19 Price to pay
20 Ethical principle linking my freedom with yours
22 Not according to plan
24 GPS suggestion
25 Soft serve alternative
26 "Notorious" SCOTUS member
27 Chex type
30 Set to simmer
32 Opposition to fixed identities, say
37 Breakout role for Ron Howard
38 Big ___ (college sports conference)
39 Source of funds for a theatre co.
40 Suprises, possibly
43 Char, as a steak
45 Vedic fire god
46 Philosophical stance associated with Derrida, Deleuze, Foucault, and Lacan
50 ___ dixit
51 Alternatively, in texts
52 Says one's piece
53 That, in Tierra del Fuego
54 Simba's vile uncle
56 Pequod captain
57 Community control
63 Dungeon restraints
64 Maine college town
65 When repeated, an all-consuming sound?
67 Bat cave covering
69 Suffix for peace
70 Robot smitten by EVE
72 Anarchistic orientation
77 Insurrectionary act
78 Thought, in Toulouse
79 Fruity quick bread
80 ___ about
81 Pitch
82 Comes out
83 Singer-songwriter Case

DOWN

1 Part of EGOT (award quartet)
2 Robot cleaner
3 Give to, as homework
4 Subdivision offerings
5 Otto meno cinque
6 Necessary: Abbr.
7 MDX and RDX, for example
8 River in Nebraska
9 Rug feature
10 Blow up: Abbr.
11 Vox populi, vox ___
12 Compound found in nuts and seeds
13 Contributing to the mix
14 Pretentiously cultured
15 Toy on a string
21 A sharp equivalent
23 Slides a card
28 Typical cinematic caper
29 Chitown to Indy dir.
30 Hokkaido city near Sapporo
31 Sue Grafton's ___ *for Noose*
33 Multilayered dessert
34 O'er opposite
35 Something to make
36 Really hurts
40 Did some surveillance
41 Wood
42 Employees, sometimes
43 Sanskrit aphorism
44 *Foucault's Pendulum* author Umberto
45 Cover story
47 Makes like a lion
48 Middle-earth kingdom
49 *The King of Staten Island* director
54 Musical Dogg
55 Distribution center pkg.
56 Type of dye
58 Banks and Pyle
59 Hang around
60 Getting to
61 Using the Internet
62 Deft pass on the court
66 It stops at Farragut North
67 Way of walking
68 Take back a typo
69 Evening, in ad speak
71 Eisenberg of *Star Trek: Deep Space Nine*
73 Yeats offering
74 Flee
75 Shark's instrument?
76 Lines on a GPS map

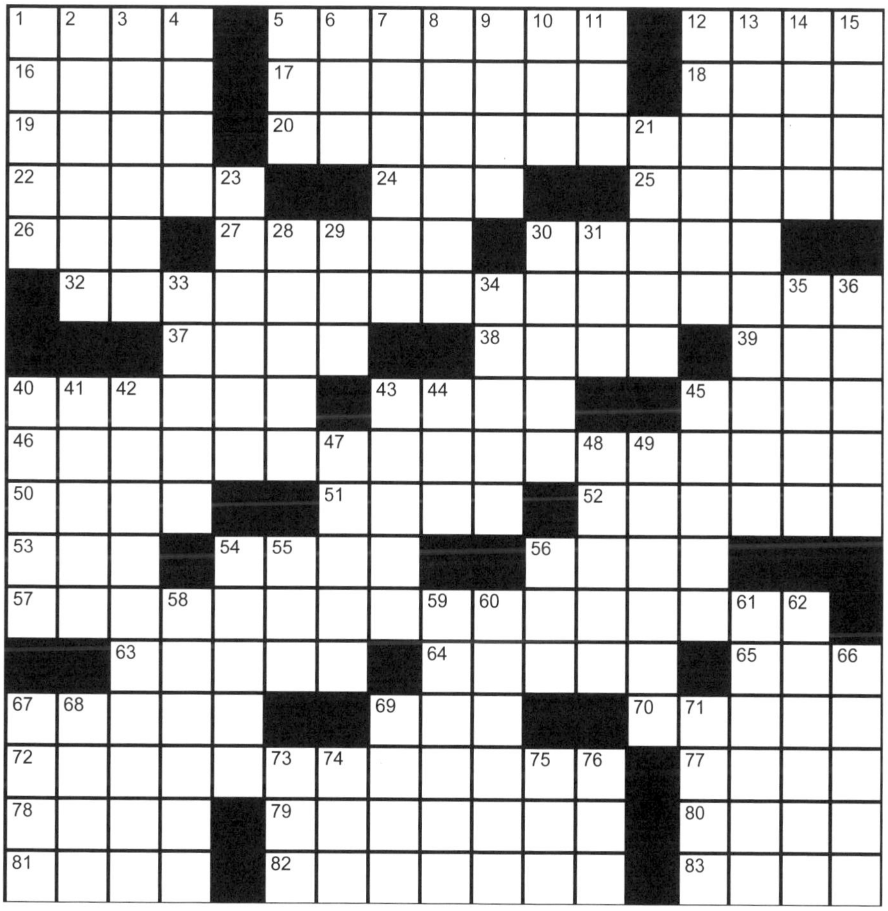

RECOGNITION

WITH GRATITUDE AND APPRECIATION FOR INDIGENOUS PEOPLES

ACROSS

1 Psych. reference
4 Cargo routes
11 Actress Ryan
14 Shout in a Greek restaurant
15 Arthurian musical
16 Charlottesville inst.
17 Cleveland (MLB)
19 Command to a canine
20 Words that up the ante
21 Unbelievable occurrence
23 Actress Carter, or the character she played on *Gimme a Break!*
24 Canadian avian
27 Eponym of the chess rating system
28 US Open champion Naomi
30 Tedious moralist
32 ___ fresca
35 Anthropologist who noted that "a small group of thoughtful, committed, citizens can change the world"
37 Something to resist?
39 Recognition for the traditional stewards of the land
44 Operatic
45 Horse of a certain color
46 Manager
47 Small opening
49 Brings before a jury
54 Young fox
56 Over again
58 "To Live and Die ___" (Shakur song)
59 12-step group for the younger crowd
62 Prototypical
64 Sass
65 Washington, DC (NFL)
68 Bear, in Bolivia
69 On the rocks
70 Pedal digit
71 ___Pen (allergic reaction treatment)
72 It might be strategic
73 Miscalculate

DOWN

1 Famous Fats
2 Cathedral features
3 Indian spice mixture
4 Bot. and bio., e.g.
5 Stand for a painter
6 Weather grp.
7 "Are ___ couple?" (relationship check)
8 College grads
9 Spiritual leader
10 ___ decisis (judicial doctrine)
11 Atlanta (MLB)
12 Vile anagram or its synonym
13 Terminal information
18 Luxe fabric
22 Rating unit for chili
25 Australian gem
26 Call for delivery
29 Famous name in cookies
31 Lady with a "Bad Romance"
33 Part of DoD
34 Telecom giant
36 Pasture parents, perhaps
38 Monthly worry for many
39 Remote batteries
40 French winery word
41 Kansas City (NFL)
42 Like most participants in tag
43 Shower attention on
48 British medical journal
50 Pussy ___ (punk band)
51 Instinctive
52 Ostrom who showed that the commons could be self-managed
53 Defensive end, on occasion
55 Like some saxophones
57 Pagan practice
59 ___ vera (succulent)
60 Speech impediment
61 Location for an icicle
63 Guitarist Atkins
66 Contender for hockey's GOAT
67 Even or even up

SOLUTION: 123, BOTTOM LEFT

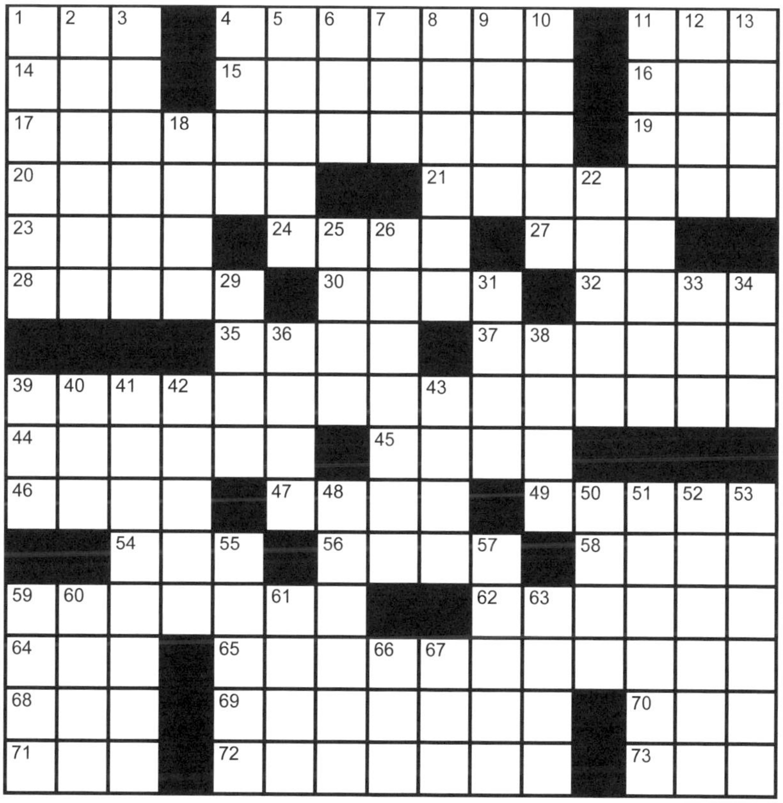

ON FERALITY

ACROSS

1 Ms. Squalor, a Lemony Snicket villain
5 Make like a lawyer and . . .
11 Fashion a dress
14 Slightly wet
15 Dance done to the 2015 hit "Watch Me"
16 Russian space station
17 Righteous Brothers classic
20 Subj. of a magazine profile
21 *48 ___* (Eddie Murphy movie)
22 Seasonal mushroom
23 Polite palindrome
25 Tasting room operator
26 Of an independent mind
31 Graphically simple
32 *Sons of Anarchy* subject
33 OPEC unit
36 Vendor of furniture and meatballs
37 Use a crowbar
38 Swerve
39 Means, in stats texts
40 Notion
42 Goes through a door
44 1957 film given the MST3k treatment
46 Zoo denizens
49 Curse
50 See 61-Across
51 Relay component
53 Last album by Janis Joplin
57 Exercises in futility
60 Successor to HST
61 With 50-Across, *The Zoo Story* playwright
62 Prefix to byte
63 "___ Blues" (track on *The Beatles*)
64 Word of defiance
65 Cardinal direction

DOWN

1 Univ. school about schools
2 Mentally together
3 Annum in the mid-22nd century
4 Posters and zines, say
5 Ogre of Japanese folklore
6 Vietnamese street food
7 Be a boo bird
8 Puts a stop to
9 Newton of the Patriots
10 Abundant
11 Sweet treat for campers
12 Duck
13 With irony
18 Slack off
19 Stretched out
24 Oohs and ___
25 Come out on top
26 ___-flam
27 Alternative to Amazon Fire
28 Females in the flock
29 Google ___ Viewer (word usage search engine)
30 11th letter
33 Une partie du drapeau tricolore
34 ___'s Bees
35 Phil of The Grateful Dead
37 Edible seed pod
38 Era admired by primitivists
40 Whole number
41 Sot's scourge
42 Author LeShan
43 One of the Oreads, say
44 Previously owned
45 Lawn care tools
46 Like some pulp fiction
47 Slur
48 More adept
51 Meteorological data
52 Actor Morales of *Ozark*
54 Kyrgyzstan's continent
55 Fed. Register contents
56 Future attorney's hurdle: Abbr.
58 Neruda wrote one to socks
59 Summer setting in Chicago: Abbr.

PREFIGURATION

FORESHADOWING THINGS TO COME

ACROSS

1 Hot winter beverage
6 Means to absolution
13 Ballpark entertainment
20 Now, to a niña
21 Clarity standard
22 Advocate, as a position
23 DIY to the max?
26 Get by (with "out")
27 ___ B. Wells, civil rights advocate
28 Diner
29 Actress Zellweger
30 Camouflage oneself
33 Small amount of ointment
35 Sporty cars
36 What we get when we work together?
44 Southwestern building material
45 "Meeeow!" (perhaps)
46 Surveils
50 9/11 first responders: Abbr.
51 Airport monitors: Abbr.
53 Some mil. hazards
55 Passes, as a law
56 Caring for those in crisis?
61 "Bloom County" penguin
62 Angkor ___
63 Meditative syllables
64 Suffix for ball
65 Fin or flipper, zoologically
68 Onetime partner of Palin
70 Force unit, on the earth's surface
72 Type of attack
74 Blood typing syst.
75 Govt. agency for retirees
76 Brewpub offering
77 Praises for picadors
79 Authentic self-government?
87 Reconciled
88 Like a skyscraper
89 Unconventional
90 Wander
92 Interpreter's lingo, sometimes
94 Raises a glass to
97 Strong scents
98 Transformative social practice?
102 Seemingly endless card game
105 Mrs., in Mexico
106 Satirist Belloc
107 *Dick Tracy* actor Ed
110 Paris's Rue de ___
114 Louvre Pyramid architect
115 Syrup source
118 Phenomenon proving that "a little rebellion now and then is a good thing"?
123 *The Waste Land* author
124 Student
125 Of the feathered kind
126 Award recipient
127 Really gets under one's skin
128 Open the door for

DOWN

1 Geological wine cellar
2 "I get it now"
3 Porter of Peru, Indiana
4 Tulsa religious inst.
5 Pooh's papa?
6 ___ curry
7 That: Sp.
8 Flagstaff campus: Abbr.
9 Lack
10 St. Petersburg river
11 Clump together
12 Style magazine
13 Nairobi natives
14 Social follower?
15 Train in the ring
16 Achy
17 Giving a sign
18 Useful talent
19 Distracted Boyfriend, et al.
24 Thought
25 Language used in Lahore
30 Site of the Ishtar Gate
31 Trim, as a chicken
32 Suffix appended to cyan
34 Hominids, for example
36 Jolt in joe, briefly
37 Bookies calculation
38 Like *The Animals* (1964)
39 Keats, for one
40 Some femmes: Abbr.
41 "Love ___" (hit for the Beatles)
42 Amy's *Baby Mama* co-star
43 © conclusion
47 Onetime Toyota brand
48 German king
49 Timberlake's band
51 Horned Frogs of the NCAA
52 Enthusiastic assent in Spanish
54 Blackthorn
57 Microbrew fav
58 Certain raptor
59 Gulf Cooperation Council member: Abbr.
60 "No more, thanks."
65 Celebrity chef Lakshmi
66 Construction girder
67 ___ plume
69 Wacko
70 Passé
71 Michelle Obama, ___ Robinson
72 According to
73 Ordinarily
75 March holiday, briefly
76 Dwight's two-time opponent
78 In fractions, what 6 is to 2 and 3: Abbr.
80 Polite reply of the past
81 Takei TV role
82 *Everything ___: A Year in the Life of My Mouth* by Tucker Shaw
83 Tesla's Musk
84 Tigris River city
85 ___ *fan tutte* (Mozart opera)
86 Talks on and on
91 WaPo, NYT, CBS, NPR, et al.
93 Do a voice over
95 Mercury astronaut
96 Short warning to an oversharer
97 Beginning to bliss?
99 Trot, say
100 Ungulates with prehensile trunks
101 180s
102 Value
103 "You ___ beautiful"
104 Children's book author Michael
108 D-Day locale
109 Evening in Saint-Étienne
111 Noxious
112 Self-cleaning appliance
113 Shakespearean monarch
115 Fit of pique
116 Palm tree noted for its berries
117 Ivy in Philly
119 McCorvey, in a famous court case
120 It's used in this clue: Abbr.
121 Date
122 Hail, to Horace

RECLAIM THE STREETS

ACROSS

1 Kasparov's affirmatives
4 Puritanical
8 Playing piano, say
14 Mod- suffix
15 Sake starter
16 Way to get coll. credit
17 Certain NCO
18 Tandoor, e.g.
19 Loosens, as laces
20 Easily graded assessment (for French 101)
23 Not temp.
24 Cooking fat
25 Lousiana brewer of Turbo-dog
28 Particularly skillful
30 Tide at the third quarter
32 Be jealous of
33 Seer (who might speak Italian sometimes)
36 Competitive channel: Abbr.
37 ___Tube
38 Grazing land
40 Application datum, often
43 Like a rude remark (perhaps in Spanish)
50 Anacondas
52 Story
53 Fusillade
54 -ish
56 Fall into a chair
58 Nobel laureate Szymborska
59 Protest participants (some speaking Esperanto)
62 Woodstock chant (not long before things turned muddy)
64 Curled feature on a pug
65 Site 2010 World Cup final, briefly
66 AOC, re Boston University
67 Pierre's pistolet
68 Workplace for an RN
69 Milton's "___ Agonistes"
70 Nutrition numbers, once: Abbr.
71 Lunar new year

DOWN

1 Sweeper's tool
2 Cheesy sauce
3 Straps in
4 Asst. ___
5 Competition
6 Republic in the north Atlantic
7 Motive, in law
8 Tense
9 Sleep disturbance
10 Leaves alone
11 Taking leave
12 Glaswegian's negative
13 Coca Cola or Sprite, e.g.
21 Like a null set
22 Cheese noted for its covering
26 Some screens, for short
27 Objectivist Rand
29 Pants part?
31 Sign on a door
34 Tía, en inglesa
35 Observes
39 Make an adjustment (to)
40 Target for crunches
41 Sticky stuff
42 Tympanum
44 ___ Crunch
45 Top performer
46 Dancer's duds
47 Put the pedal to the metal
48 How to serve some cocktails
49 Hollows from within, say
51 Cooks, in a way
55 Protein component, briefly
57 ___ donna
60 Biblical masturbator
61 Pub offerings
62 Lil ___ X, noted for "Old Town Road"
63 Rock-___ (classic jukebox brand)

1	2	3		4	5	6	7		8	9	10	11	12	13
14				15					16					
17				18					19					
20			21				22							
23					24				25			26	27
28			29		30		31		32				
33				34				35		36			
		37					38		39				
40	41	42		43		44	45	46			47	48	49
50			51		52				53				
54				55		56			57		58		
		59			60				61				
62	63					64				65			
66						67				68			
69						70				71			

STRATEGIC DISRUPTION

There's a time when the operation of the machine becomes so odious, makes you so sick at heart, that you can't take part! You can't even passively take part! And you've got to put your bodies upon the gears and upon the wheels . . . upon the levers, upon all the apparatus, and you've got to make it stop! —Mario Savio (1964)

ACROSS

1 Step on a ladder
5 Dire, as a situation
10 Archeological find
18 Qatari ruler
19 Ewok residence
20 Role in producing an anthology
21 *Marx analyzed its laws of motion
22 Brief bit of a polite request
24 Away from the wind
26 Wagnerian heroine
27 *Ukases, for instance
33 Make breakfast, maybe
35 Professional's wages
37 LOTR actor Holm
38 Segregationist Arkansas governor Faubus
41 Singer whose albums are *19*, *21*, & *25*
42 Middle of the second quarter
45 *Folsom or Sing Sing
47 Place of residence
49 Titter sound
50 Abnormal swelling
52 Andean camelids
54 *Source of stratification
58 Reapers
62 Lovable pup
64 Second of a Latin I conjugation trio
68 Request for Chinese takeout
69 *Afflication of type A personalities

72 Corinthian cheer
73 Beethoven tributee
75 Nail file material
77 Losing tic-tac-toe row
78 Illinois River city
79 Poetry presentation
81 *Problematic approach to policing
86 Hatha yoga pose
88 Very long skirt
90 Craven, master of horror
91 *Ecologically detrimental practice
99 Slowly leaks
100 21 phrase
101 State firmly
102 Pens and paints supplier
103 Surveil
104 News story start

DOWN

1 Videocam button
2 Thurman of Hollywood
3 Puppy bite
4 The flu, once
5 Understands
6 Genetic messenger
7 Dwight's opponent, twice
8 There it is!
9 Celtic tongue
10 Play division
11 Wade antagonist in a court case
12 Whodunit character, in slang

13 They're exchanged at a wedding
14 Gala wear
15 When to meet for a late lunch
16 French coiner of "sociology"
17 "___ I may . . ." (no matter the effort)
23 ___ City (building sets)
25 Schiaparelli and Klensch of fashion fame
27 More than irritated
28 Bird with something to say
29 Replied to an invitation, briefly
30 Carpenter's groove
31 Kagan on the Court
32 Ripken in the Baseball Hall of Fame
33 Bass, e.g.
34 Hellas, in other words
36 Brings in, as a harvest
39 "Whose woods these ___ think . . ." (Frost)
40 Peruvian capital
42 Comfy shoe
43 1990 civil rights law: Abbr.
44 Notable prog rock band
46 Student's concerns
48 Thermometer type
51 European peak
53 University of the Punjab setting
55 "Golly!"
56 Steel mill need

57 Good soil
58 ___-cone (shaved ice treat)
59 Stealthily acquire
60 Singer Sumac
61 Parfait feature
63 Parisienne's boyfriend
65 Recipe direction
66 "Sing ___"
67 Industrial effect
70 Russian poet Mandelshtam
71 Prepare to fight again
74 Mauna ___
76 Connecticut Ivy
78 David Bowie album of covers
80 Like swamps, say
81 Ronald : Nancy :: Mikhail : ___
82 Voice of Fredricksen in *Up*
83 West Point student
84 Yellow spring flower
85 L for Livy
87 Type of prof.
89 Sounds of relief
90 Small bird
92 As well
93 Work by Karel Capek
94 Suffix for a resident
95 First of a Latin I conjugation trio
96 "___ Been Everywhere" (country song)
97 Nickname for Stark, Lord of Winterfell
98 Pre-doc test

GRAFFITI

RADICAL THOUGHTS FROM MAY 1968

ACROSS

1 Poses, as a question
5 Zoloft marketer
11 Ducks and geese
15 Sibilant call for attention
19 Spaces for sheep
20 In the last month
21 Tech device introduced in 2001
22 Somewhat startled greeting
23 With 71-Across, a political thought?
25 Sci. of the biome
26 Lacking fat
27 Spanish "Listen!"
28 Zooms (by)
29 Composer Satie
30 Salad green
31 Posh house
33 With 43-Across, an economic thought?
39 When doubled, Peruvian beans and rice dish
41 Prefix for business or culture
42 Crossed (out)
43 See 33-Across
50 Exasperated comment
52 Bit of Morse code
53 "That's tasty!"
54 German political unit
55 Pitch on a roof
56 JFK's predecessor
58 Washer's capacity
61 Group profiled in *Straight Outta Compton*
62 Syndicate for newspaper features
65 Tea-drinker's latte
68 Temps helping parents
71 See 23-Across
74 Battery output
75 German grocery chain
76 Lying comfortably
78 College in Cedar Rapids
79 Lightly blacken, in cooking
81 Didn't fast
82 Chem., e.g.
83 Eponymous list owner
86 ___Kosh B'gosh (kids' apparel brand)
88 Native Spanish speaker, in school: Abbr.
90 Port on the Loire
93 With 101-Across, a social thought?
98 Sharers' pronoun
99 Flatbread baked in a tandoor
100 Makes after taxes
101 See 93-Across
106 Title for a bishop: Abbr.
110 Version of 21-Across, 2005–2017
111 Source of eye color
112 Bah-Kho-Je tribe, a.k.a. the *ayuwa* ("sleepy ones")
114 Manning of the Giants
115 Fastener
116 Get or grasp
117 An idiosyncratic thought?
121 Confront, as one's failings
122 Don't ___ (no arguments please)
123 Woeful feeling
124 Ratatouille or goulash
125 Quipsters
126 Helpful spots: Abbr.
127 Residents on visas
128 Georgia and Ukraine, once

DOWN

1 *Tuesdays with Morrie* author
2 "Later, dude."
3 Stereotypical angry, privileged, white woman
4 Ship's heading: Abbr.
5 Woolly Hungarian herding dog
6 Drinking game
7 "No lie!"
8 Sometime source of teen trauma
9 Brit. recording label
10 Mythical bird of prey
11 Diner denizen on TV
12 Work previously referenced: Abbr.
13 Chewbacca from Kashyyyk
14 Type of cholesterol, briefly
15 Spotted pattern
16 ___ Madness (long-running comedic play)
17 Fracking rock
18 Pitchfork part
24 Angel of death
29 Be instructive
32 ___ *Oprah Magazine*
34 Pacific surfing destination
35 Execs
36 Cava de ___ (tequila brand)
37 Date on a bag of dates: Abbr.
38 Matches a bet
40 Bottles of beer
43 Back-to-back-to-back titles
44 That is: Lat.
45 ___ mania (17th century bubble)
46 Ins. provider
47 Rountable members
48 University in Appleton, Wisc.
49 When planes are due: Abbr.
50 How generic drugs are sold: Abbr.
51 Fanatical
57 Beats poet?
59 Good thing
60 Fill, as a prescription
63 ___, amas, amat
64 Spotted, like Tweety Bird
65 Animation collectible
66 Laid low
67 Friend, in Avignon
69 Chuck Rocha's ___ *Bernie: The Inside Story of How Bernie Sanders Brought Latinos Into the Political Revolution*
70 Network for "Full Frontal with Samantha Bee"
72 Like some punishments
73 Toothbrush brand
74 750, in ancient Rome
77 Active-duty types: Abbr.
80 NY representative in "The Squad"
84 Some are radioactive
85 Wildebeests
87 Sticks around
88 Like a French peer
89 Infamous filmmaker Riefenstahl
91 Off the path of virtue, say
92 Treetop sight
94 Tolkien creature
95 Concert memorabilia
96 Gaelic negative
97 Quaint ball game
101 Tropical veranda
102 Ordain, as a policy
103 Appealing fragrance
104 Mag and Air Force 1
105 Terra ___
107 Musical breaks

SOLUTION: 124, BOTTOM RIGHT

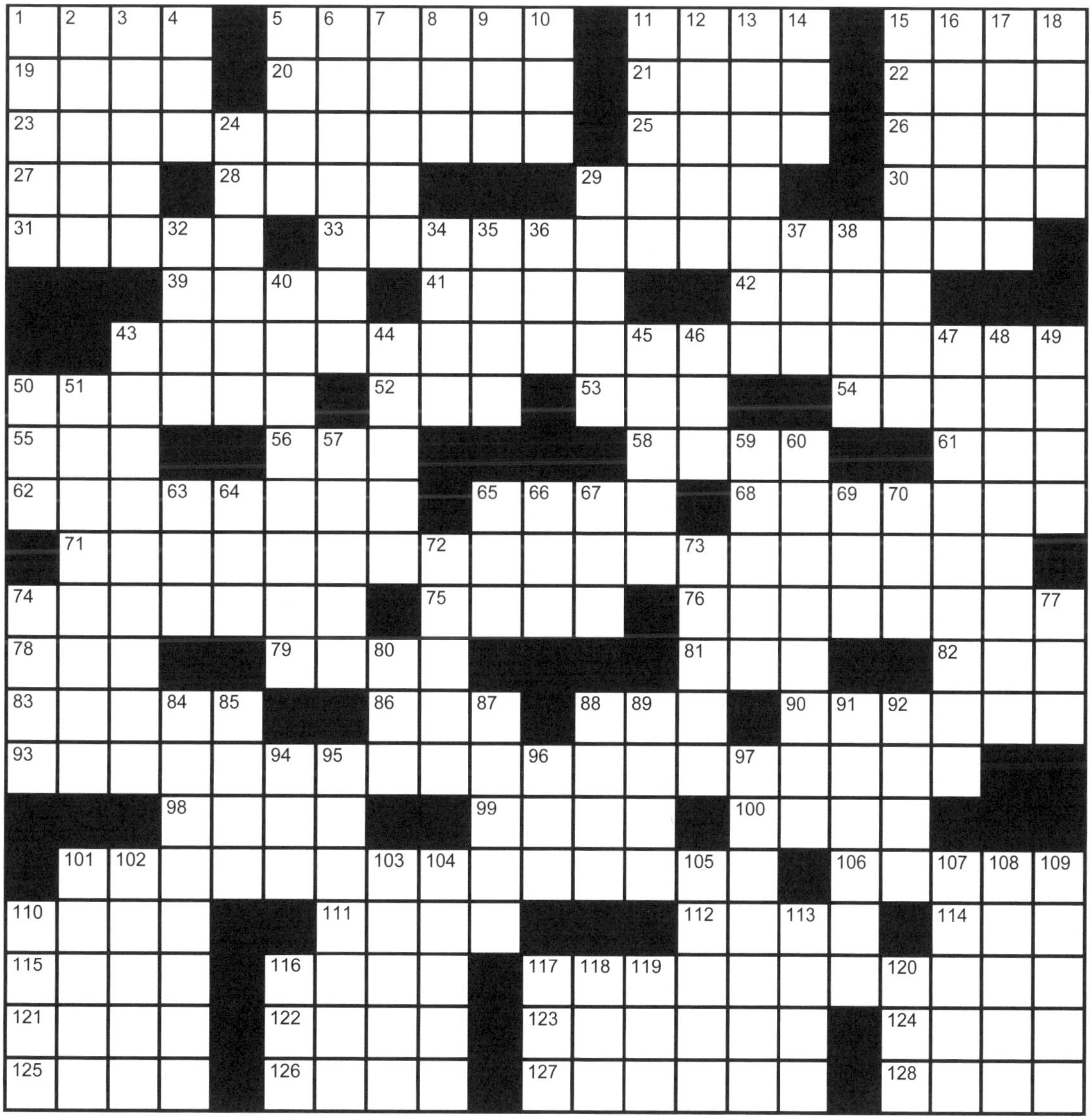

108 Antagonist for Bugs
109 Contents of an op-ed page
110 Sign of a problematic URL
113 Counterparts to wherefores
116 Cumberland, for example
117 Power suffix?
118 Scrub
119 Serpent in hieroglyphics
120 Mag. subscription component

DEMOCRACY IN THE WORKPLACE

DEMOCRACY CAN BE DISRUPTIVE

ACROSS

1 Hobo
4 Dismissive interjection
7 Philosopher Lao-___
10 Make a note of (down)
13 Garten of cookbook fame
14 Low poker hand
16 Hasbro card game
17 Yossarian's friend, in *Catch-22*
18 Cloverleaf parts
19 Protein source
20 Where Homer naps?
23 Trojan War story
24 Major concept of 7-Across
25 Pet food brand
28 Color on Monopoly deeds
29 Where ___? (orientation inquiry)
31 Othello's lieutenant
33 Project requirements
35 Vichyssoise ingredients
36 Seat store?
40 Sudden attack
41 Problem treated by a CPAP machine
42 Bodega owner
44 Yes, aboard ship
45 Filled tortilla
49 ___ packing (kicked out)
50 Have a bite
52 Liverpool FC star
53 Romeo y Julieta in Havana?
57 German interjection
59 Pennsylvania Railroad city
60 *Curb Your Enthusiasm* presenter
61 Sweetheart, in slang
62 Indigenous Alaskans
63 First rate
64 Sunscreen datum
65 Observe, perhaps discreetly
66 Mercedes models
67 ___-cones (icy treats)

DOWN

1 Cyborg-like
2 Like some crowds
3 Oft-intoned *The Brady Bunch* name
4 Expressed disapproval
5 Kendrick, of *Pitch Perfect*
6 Mister in München
7 Home to Rays and Bucs
8 Plastic bag brand
9 Major or Minor constellation
10 "Hold on!"
11 Lennon's "Plastic ___ Band" album
12 Catnip mouse, say
15 Radical democratic essence
21 IT concern
22 George Takei, for one
26 ___ & Ike (candy)
27 Initial request for help
29 Bonobo, e.g.
30 Self-referential, in a way
32 Start to a phonetic alphabet
33 Scottish Terrier cousin
34 PlayStation producer
36 Rent
37 Competitive cooking show
38 Mescals and saguaros
39 User ___ (highway tolls, e.g.)
40 NFL scoring options
43 Seriously?
45 Body art, in brief
46 Maui greetings
47 C in Organic Chemistry?
48 "Imagine" song
51 Shaw of jazz fame
52 Sings like Ella, say
54 Boarding pass info
55 Really low clouds
56 Indigo dye source
57 Six-pack components
58 Newsboy, e.g.

SOLUTION: 125, TOP LEFT

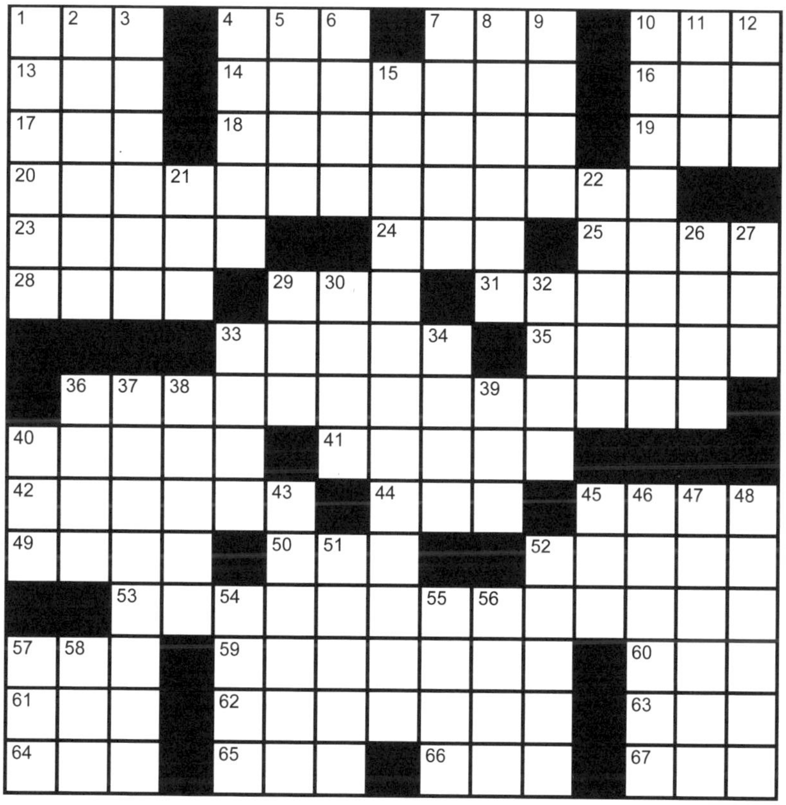

TRANSGRESSING BOUNDARIES

BREAK ON THROUGH TO THE OTHER SIDE

ACROSS

1 Patriarchy's beneficiaries

4 Sandbars

10 OCR product

14 Hail, to Caesar

15 Tool in a marimbist's hand

16 West Coast gas brand

17 1985 Glenn Close/Jeff Bridges thriller

19 Seriously injure

20 La ___ (famous opera house)

21 *Full House* star

23 POTUS in the 1950's

24 Six years, for a Senator

26 Sister of Laertes

28 Steppes setting

30 Path traced by a lob shot

33 One way to stand

34 Laramie, Wyoming, once

38 Storage can

39 Return to a prior lesson

40 Affectedly modest

43 Herding dog breed

45 Summary account

48 Noir classic

49 Restaurant review app

50 Provide consent for

53 Game show mogul Griffin

55 Links org.

56 Main character in *The Metamorphosis*

59 Wine center of Tuscany

62 Authors, metaphorically

64 Center of volcanic activity

66 Ontario neighbor

67 Watch retronym

68 "The Greatest"

69 Exam for a future JD

70 Uses as a stool

71 Danson of *The Good Place*

DOWN

1 Sr. officers in the USMC

2 Brief rescue mission

3 Dialectical move

4 Unfounded allegation

5 Ate for dinner, say

6 Bravos in Barcelona's Camp Nou

7 Pie ___ mode

8 Kids' blocks brand

9 Soak, as tea leaves

10 Sanders who hosts *It's Been a Minute*

11 Baby bed

12 Not basic

13 Vegan's credo

18 Gather, in a gradual manner

22 "Baba O'Riley" band

25 Author of *American Scripture*

27 White-tailed sea bird

28 @ (symbolically)

29 Acapulco affirmative

31 No longer active: Abbr.

32 Street ___

35 Metaphor and metonymy

36 The Way, in Eastern thought

37 Philosopher known for his "razor"

40 Adept

41 Artistic medium

42 Clipped affirmation

43 Dear one, in modern slang

44 Chicago's ___ Opera company

45 Vertically descend

46 *The Captain and the Glory* author

47 Skulls

51 Small plates in Seville

52 Gulf state citizen

54 Ink, virtually

57 Ella Fitzgerald's specialty

58 Feels unwell

60 Div. for the Mets

61 Assistance

63 Ready

65 ___ Fighters

POST-ANARCHIST TENDENCIES

ANARCHIST TO THE END

ACROSS

1 Imprudent
5 Potentially unbridgeable divide
10 Splinter group
14 ___ mater
15 Winfrey's production studio
16 Earthen stewpot
17 Foodie's reference
20 Paperback writer
21 View from the valley
22 Combination form for "height"
24 Café au ___
25 Hypothesis
30 School with a Carbondale campus: Abbr.
31 Wide shoe abbr.
32 Fourpence piece, once
34 "Gotcha, man."
36 Mini, e.g.
39 Rec center abbr.
40 Cowboy competition
42 Dove's cry
43 Tuna type
44 Clockwork
49 Former home for the Mets
50 Enthusiastic flair
51 Sweet corn option
55 "...do ___ and establish this Constitution"
59 Reading group
61 Environmental sci.
62 Traffic jam
63 Horserace margin, at times
64 Portrayer of Sparrow and Wonka
65 Mississippi feature
66 Small pest

DOWN

1 Shankar specialty
2 Family name for MLB's Jesús, Matty, and Felipe
3 Porn
4 Sarcastic laughter
5 Stone fruit
6 Porkpie, e.g.
7 Shape of many monuments
8 Had gone bad: Brit.
9 Cash, in slang
10 Tale told to get sympathy
11 Beings in *The Time Machine*
12 Lump of dirt
13 Hot ___ (provocative commentary)
18 Ridicule
19 Light on a film set
23 Short run
25 Black ___
26 Pen name for Marie Louise de la Ramée
27 Insurer known for wry ads
28 Cicero, say
29 USS Sequoia, for example
30 Rapper ___ Mix-a-Lot (a.k.a. Anthony Ray)
33 Mai ___
35 Checks out eHow
37 *Bush's Brain* subject
38 Skater's moves
41 Yellowish tone
45 Mythical sorceress
46 People indigenous to Aotearoa (a.k.a. New Zealand)
47 Caesar's Antony
48 Denouement
51 Type of TV display
52 Not naughty, on Santa's list
53 Sports car roof option
54 Tournament passes
56 Vast time span
57 "___ thing" (actual phenomenon)
58 Russian refusal
60 File for damages

SOCIAL ECOLOGY

ACROSS

1 Priors, in a way
7 Rabbi's religion
14 Prep a mummy
20 Sign up
21 MA or PA
22 Technician on tour?
23 Pest
24 How social ecologists keep it together?
26 Conclude
27 Takes it easy
29 Interrogatory seeking confirmation
30 Di Caprio, briefly
31 Saved, as a souvenir
32 Biblical mount
33 Jay coming out at night?
34 How social ecologists keep it local?
39 Deceive
42 Toyota sedan model
43 Feature of akpress.org
44 Hoosier astronaut known as "Gus"
48 Wonka creator
49 Gainsay
50 With 77-Across, bots with benefits for social ecologists?
53 Challenge for a beginning guitarist
56 Emergency vehicle sounds
57 Biography of Chicago 7 attorney Weinglass
58 Early analgesic
61 Condemns
62 Northeast Corridor train
64 Holistic approach for social ecologists
69 Crimson Crisp, for one
70 Allocates (with "out")
71 Cake eponym
72 School support grp.
73 Stated a view
75 Brews, as tea
77 See 70-Across
80 Wild hog
81 Seeks damages from
85 "Oh yeah?!"
86 Role in a play
87 Solidarność city
89 "Ready or not, here ___"
91 Abundance of anarchy for social ecologists?
93 ¿Como ___ usted?
96 Empaneled ones
98 RPI component: Abbr.
99 Hmong neighbor
100 Officials recording the game
102 Particular skill
104 Will Smith & Tommy Lee Jones film: Abbr.
107 Sage for social ecologists
110 Like a crescent
112 Puzzle
113 Cooking instruction
114 *Good Times* Rolle
115 Grape along the Garonne
116 Consent
117 Concert merch

DOWN

1 Nota ___
2 Informed about, as a plan
3 Yankees slugger, to fans
4 Turf to transplant
5 Artist in a Toledo museum
6 Turn off the alarm
7 Equitable
8 Applications
9 FiOS alternative
10 Initially
11 2001 Sean Penn film
12 Way up
13 Cray cray
14 Segue in logic
15 ___ & Chandon (champagne maker)
16 Emeril's interjection
17 Singer who started with "19"
18 Closet contents
19 #___ (anti-harassment movement)
25 Immunology therapeutic
28 Motor-oil additive
31 Tarantino martial arts series
32 Mount ___ (Andy Griffith hometown)
33 Puzzling TV series set on an island
34 Magazine produced by "the usual gang of idiots"
35 Charlottesville sch.
36 Slangy negative
37 Dell competitor
38 Come down
40 Goes astray
41 La hermana de mi madre
45 Sunshine in Port-au-Prince
46 Threatening words
47 Hello ___ is
49 Word to a toddler
50 Some museum guards?
51 1963 film ___ la Douce
52 Top of the line
54 First Nation people of western Canada
55 Reflex sound
56 Repaired a shoe, in a way
58 Turns a book into a film, say
59 Be social at a social, possibly
60 Institution headquartered in Vatican City
61 Big name in Chicago politics
62 Grp. of seniors
63 Impressive person
65 Unique prefix
66 Subj. of Article I of the Constitution
67 Computer operator
68 Actress Issa of *Insecure*
73 Odometer start?
74 Good gig
75 Categorize
76 Body designs, briefly
78 First Chinese dynasty
79 MoMA's location
80 Ale brand with a triangle logo
82 Loughborough, e.g. (location for the Anarchism Research Group)
83 The e in i.e.
84 Backdrop for balloons
86 Stuttgart sports car name
87 Challenge: Var.
88 Author of *The Butter Battle Book*
90 International soccer league
91 Sow to sell
92 Geometric fig.
93 Fudd with a firearm
94 Hot house?
95 Doughnuts, say
97 Structural change, in brief
100 People of the Arctic region
101 One of four colors
102 Dictatorial command
103 No longer fooled by
104 Certain tuna
105 Road to Rome
106 Kreischer of stand-up comedy
108 O-line personnel
109 Tee follower?
111 Ultimate degree

ESSENTIAL EGOISM

WISDOM FROM MAX STIRNER

ACROSS

1 Aleutian island
5 Walks nervously
10 Prop for Sherlock Holmes
14 He played Harvey in *Milk*
15 Lyric muse
16 Away from the harbor
17 Egoist observation, part 1
20 Post-fight charge, possibly
21 Prep school for English royalty
22 Prefix with logical
23 Work with a book
26 Egoist observation, part 2
33 Hermano de Fidel
34 Statutes
35 Millennial year, in film credits
36 Tiny to a tot
37 Egoist observation, part 3
39 Enter
40 Studio location
41 Sit in a tub
42 Old Norse character
43 Egoist observation, part 4
48 Not at all nice
49 Singer-songwriter Brickell
50 Window part
53 Like high-school kids
57 Egoist observation, part 5
61 Cooked and ready to eat
62 Of eagles and egrets
63 Jazz great "Fatha" Hines
64 Shadow box, say
65 Sites for squirrels
66 Toward the harbor

DOWN

1 Turkmenistan locale
2 Assam and Darjeeling
3 Wool caps in the Highlands
4 In prejudicial manner
5 Prepared potatoes
6 Schoolyard retort
7 Half-___ (latte order)
8 *L'___ et le Néant* (Sartre opus)
9 Fireplace residue
10 *Parks and Recreation* place
11 Kinda, sorta
12 Pod vegetable
13 "___ the rich!"
18 1960s German activist Dutschke
19 Early AMs
24 Under ___ (sports apparel company)
25 Van Morrison hit
26 Some Republicans
27 MiLB's Springfield Cardinals
28 "___ been the wind" (explanation for a door slam)
29 Like a ditz
30 ___ milk
31 Great Powers conflict: Abbr.
32 Thinner, as a pen point
37 Outplayed an opponent
38 Quiche Lorraine ingredient
39 Hot healthy drink
41 Egyptian peninsula
44 Lent closing
45 Furbaby
46 Old theaters
47 Wittgenstein's birthplace
51 MRI, for example
52 Possess
54 ___ Sea (shrinking Kazakhstan lake)
55 "Hellboy" feature
56 Reese's role in *Legally Blonde*
57 MS count
58 Move like a roo
59 De Armas, *Knives Out* actress
60 Sue Grafton's ___ *for Noose*

PERMACULTURE

PRINCIPLES OF ETHICAL GARDENING

ACROSS

1 Short story writer Babel
6 PIN pad sites
10 Dens for draughts and darts
14 Generic email closing
16 Draftable
17 Assemble soil, sun, and water
19 Chiwere-speaking people
20 Gouda alternative
21 Decorative circle
22 Serling who created *The Twilight Zone*
23 Browser segment
24 Grp. noted for a 1974 kidnapping
25 Be efficient
31 Obedient sort
32 Town in a Hersey title
33 Type of meat, à la carte
34 Occupy ___ (mutual aid effort after a NY hurricane)
36 Helvetica, say
40 Savory jelly
42 Printer filler
43 Embrace companion planting
47 Western hemisphere grp.
48 Org. for the Crew and the Union
49 It's ___-win situation
50 Educational institution
52 "Highway to Hell" band
53 Parapsychological power
56 Practice sustainability
59 *Pictures ___ Exhibition* (classic prog rock album)
60 Like many gift cards
61 San ___, Italy
62 Active volcano in the Philippines (anagram of "alta")
63 Sketches

DOWN

1 Shakespearean schemer
2 Window blinds component
3 Nina Simone, for example
4 Part of NCAA: Abbr.
5 Put on a happy face
6 Scour
7 Abound
8 Editorial workload: Abbr.
9 Passenger in hiding
10 Dermal aperture
11 Like a part without a player
12 Ladybird
13 Fierce alter ego for Beyoncé?
15 Triage specialist, briefly
18 ___ Dictionary (guide to modern slang)
23 Mary Lincoln, née ___
25 Sony handheld, for short
26 Greek letter that looks like P
27 Aloft, in "The Star-Spangled Banner"
28 Bespoke item on a laptop
29 Country folk artist Griffith
30 Remote traps?
34 Make explicit
35 ___ Quilt (NAMES Project memorial)
37 Popular nail polish brand
38 Court feature
39 Hear a case in court
41 Greater than the ___ its parts
42 "Do go on."
43 Annul, as a court judgment
44 Religious retreat
45 Poet Lindsay
46 Concluded
47 Wilde man of writing?
51 Prefix related to wine
52 Gillette razor brand
53 Humorous Bombeck
54 Hasenpfeffer, for one
55 Many academicians: Abbr.
57 Cellular polymer
58 ___ Lingus (carrier to Dublin)

TRANSVALUATION OF VALUES

MAKE THAT TRANS*VALUATION

ACROSS

1 Southwestern tablelands
6 Wanders around
10 Self-referential
14 Southwestern flavoring
15 See 1-Down
16 Avant-garde composer Satie
17 Certain nonbeliever
18 See 32-Across
19 Like Arp's work
20 *Expats?
23 Does demanding work
24 Take in a course
25 At sea
28 Ethiopian language
32 With 18-Across, "Jive Talkin'" group
33 *Alter your exam prep?
36 Fifth book of the New Testament
38 Key for Unicode symbols
39 Major or majorly
40 *Remodel part of the clothing store?
45 Like some photo prints: Abbr.
46 Prince in both Homer and Shakespeare
47 Make an accusation
49 Legal thing
50 City on the Red River
52 *Aim of abolishing heterosexism
58 Department with limited horizons, figuratively
59 ___ Soul (hip-hop trio)
60 Smartphone, on occasion
61 Ntozake Shange's *For Colored Girls Who Have Considered Suicide / When the Rainbow Is* ___
62 Mummy's chamber
63 Notable Rosenberg
64 CNN's Blitzer
65 Mount in Thessaly
66 "Go Tell Aunt ___" (Americana tune)

DOWN

1 Vs. 15-Across, landmark 4th Amendment case
2 French peer?
3 Multi-generational narrative
4 Streamlined Studebaker of old
5 Given a red card
6 *Dead Souls* author
7 Audible interruptions
8 Per ___
9 "What are you going to do about it?"
10 Contemplate
11 Part of QED
12 Uncluttered
13 Prelude to a pseudonym
21 Name on a bank card
22 Slangy declinations
25 Toward the stern
26 Interior design
27 Old, but new again
28 Basic drawing course
29 Kolkata currency
30 Picking out of a lineup, say
31 Soak or rinse
34 Noir noisemakers
35 Last of a series: Abbr.
37 Stoli competitor
41 Went on the lam
42 "Remember when . . ."
43 When repeated, an Orkan farewell
44 Boastful winner
48 Neuwirth role on *Frasier*
50 Navigates and steers
51 Jordanian city or gulf
52 Philly cheesesteak name
53 Anarchist author of *The Technological Society*
54 Some vintage autos
55 Prelude to a take: Abbr.
56 Ready to drive
57 Annually: Abbr.
58 Use needle and thread

1	2	3	4	5		6	7	8	9		10	11	12	13
14						15					16			
17						18					19			
20					21					22				
			23						24					
25	26	27						28				29	30	31
32				33		34	35							
36			37			38					39			
40				41	42				43	44		45		
46									47		48			
			49				50	51						
	52	53				54						55	56	57
58					59					60				
61					62					63				
64					65					66				

INTEGRATED LABOR

Highlighting the 1899 book discussing "the advantages which civilised societies could derive from a combination of industrial pursuits with intensive agriculture, and of brain work with manual work."

ACROSS

1 Summer setting: Abbr.
4 Thinker with incompleteness theorems
9 Garciaparra in the Red Sox Hall of Fame
14 Mozart's ego
15 Stunned
16 Grammy-winning Mary J.
17 With 60-Across, what Goodwill Industries operates
19 Holiday tune
20 Audible kiss
21 It's turned
23 Gramps' counterpart
24 App for a flash mob
26 Prepare in oil
28 Cancel
29 Places for batters and batteries
33 Banksy's "Kissing Coppers," say
34 Carnival city
35 Locomotive power source
36 Anarchist author of the work alluded to in this puzzle
39 Oktoberfest container
41 Old time curse
42 ___ *You My Mother?* (children's book)
45 Hershey and Jelly Belly facilities
49 HBO competitor
50 Church founded by Richard Allen
51 Summertime wear
52 Lowry who authored *The Giver*
54 Salon sound
57 Game for kids in a car
58 *Full House* twins
60 See 17-Across
63 Pal, on Talk Like a Pirate Day
64 ___ *of Two Cities*
65 Word with Agnus or Opus
66 Musée d'___ (Paris museum)
67 Words of self-congratulation
68 New Left org.

DOWN

1 Put down
2 Bagel topping
3 North America and Europe, for some
4 Software development company
5 Penny word
6 Unlit, as an alley
7 Actor Bremner of *Wonder Woman*
8 Went first
9 Peacock network: Abbr.
10 *The Good Earth* heroine
11 Word of warning?
12 Political theory associated with Chantal Mouffe
13 Chill
18 Overdue
22 Rubbed cuts
24 CEO degree
25 Complement and compliment, for example
27 Tumbler brand
30 Backtalk
31 Back scrubber
32 Deighton, author of *The IPCRESS File*
36 Jennings of *Jeopardy!* fame
37 Rapper Flo ___
38 Twitch
39 Studious type
40 Practitioners of wu wei
42 Bluetooth accessories
43 Corrected a textual error
44 Solidarity start?
46 Onetime home for 9-Across
47 "It makes sense now."
48 ___ Hashanah
49 Sort of replay, briefly
53 "Did you ever ___ goose . . ." (Raffi lyric)
55 Slightest amount
56 Entreat
59 Bronx team on chyrons
61 Airline whose hub is AMS
62 Auntie, to Mom or Dad

DESTABILIZING HIERARCHIES

LIBERATION IS NO EASY WALK (NOR IS THIS AN EASY PUZZLE)

ACROSS

1 Six-pack contents?
4 Plug of tobacco
8 "You say you want a revolution," for example
13 Center of Chicago
15 Misplace
16 High-end Honda
17 Data
18 Yemeni, say
19 ___ *Secretary* (Téa Leoni series)
20 Hypes
22 Sign of twins?
23 Actor Washington and baller Thomas
24 Bum, to a Brit
25 Music store?
26 Tax system beloved by Libertarians
30 Possess
33 Eyes: Lat.
35 L'États-Unis, par exemple
36 Smoothie berry
37 Vacation rental
38 Compulsion
39 Give for a time
40 ___ way (at all)
41 Went over the limit
42 Kegger lure
44 Sweetie
46 Small annoyances
47 Bureaucratic annoyance
51 Loquacious
54 Some Comic Con collectibles
55 Adar celebration
56 *Harry Potter* prop
57 "Pumping Up with ___ & Franz" (SNL sketch)
58 Anxious stress
59 Cutting ___
60 Pinot potable
61 Tiny sea creature
62 Roe, for example
63 Birth certificate datum

DOWN

1 Defense mechanism?
2 Something extra
3 Film director Coppola
4 Caste + struggle (mondegreen)
5 Falcon-headed Egyptian god
6 Right away: Abbr.
7 Arachnid architecture
8 Most uninspiring
9 Racial superiority (invert)
10 Fashion designer Gernreich
11 Islamic Republic on the Gulf
12 Lingerie item, for short
14 Self-appointed enforcers of norms (transpose)
21 Pa
22 Male and female (anagram)
24 Huge poker bet
26 Completely messed up, in slang
27 Lobby for the Medicare-eligible
28 Buster Brown's dog (seemingly named for a cat)
29 Stricken (with "out")
30 ___-caf (latte order)
31 Taiwanese PC brand
32 Stereotypical barn topper
34 Walking aids
43 Image format
45 Woodworking tool
47 Grassland for grazing
48 *Hadestown* creator Mitchell
49 Popular pasta
50 Colchester's county
51 Device for sleep apnea sufferers: Abbr.
52 Venezuelan politician Chávez
53 Type of seed cover
54 Style in a barber's repertoire
56 Brought together

TAG, YOU'RE IT!

ONLY CONNECT

ACROSS

1 Biblical land
5 1956 Marilyn Monroe film
12 Shrek, for one
16 Actor's request for a cue
17 ___ Riot (media collective)
18 Board game Prof.
19 Provide sustenance to
20 Kiln product
21 Tire type
22 Gallup competitor
24 Quadrennial event to protest: Abbr.
25 Action figure, in relation to a movie
26 Chai, e.g.
29 Taken aboard a UFO
32 ___-haw (donkey's bray)
33 Ind. neighbor
34 Stepped (on)
35 CIA forerunner
36 Type type
37 Long time
39 Vaping instrument, briefly
42 Klingon speaker
46 Bay Area campus, briefly
50 Member of the peerage
51 Formal afterthoughts
52 Part of RPG
53 Like this puzzle's subject
55 Max Stirner's *The ___ and Its Own*
56 Something to make?
58 Noted NYC Rep. in DC
59 ___ angle
61 Voilà!
63 Mauna ___
64 Word in a Turgenev title
65 Broadway production
66 Traffic citation
69 Breakfast tray item
73 ___ majeste
74 Rugby term
78 "The Doctor ___"
80 Type type
83 Backtalk
84 He adored Roxanne
86 Scrubbing pad brand
87 Condition for TV's Monk
88 Translucent plastic
89 Tormentor
90 Onetime auto make
91 Gilbert and Kagan

DOWN

1 Mischievous
2 English Channel resort town
3 Infant attire
4 French wine region
5 Tampa Bay player
6 One along the Oise
7 Shakespearean term of contempt (ironically to modern ears)
8 MRI, for example
9 Certain prowler
10 "Either that wallpaper goes ___ do" (Oscar Wilde's last words, so they say)
11 ___ Park, home of the Pirates
12 Part of FIOS
13 Bind, in a way
14 Birthstones for a few Leos
15 Perfects
23 Interstate sight
25 Swagger, on the street
27 Game of Xs and Os
28 Modern b'day greeting
30 Hair style
31 Competitive, in a way
36 PC scrolling key
38 Certain
39 ___ Martell, *Game of Thrones* princess
40 Fashionable Chanel
41 ___-Z (classic Camaro)
43 Idyllic spots
44 Party requisite, often
45 Ship speed units
47 Crower
48 Change direction abruptly
49 Topping for a Greek salad
54 "All ___ is for a little respect"
57 Harley, in slang
60 Farm residents?
62 Attention-getting guttural sound
66 Popular tropical fish
67 To repeat . . .
68 Instruments in the string section
70 Mythological enchantress
71 Bolt of Olympic fame
72 Noted colonial transport
73 Owning the ___ (troll's goal)
75 Shoe type
76 Author of *The Vampire Chronicles*
77 Certain prom style
79 Negative votes
81 They, in Toulouse
82 Simple bed
84 The Cavs, on a crawl
85 Brynner of old Hollywood

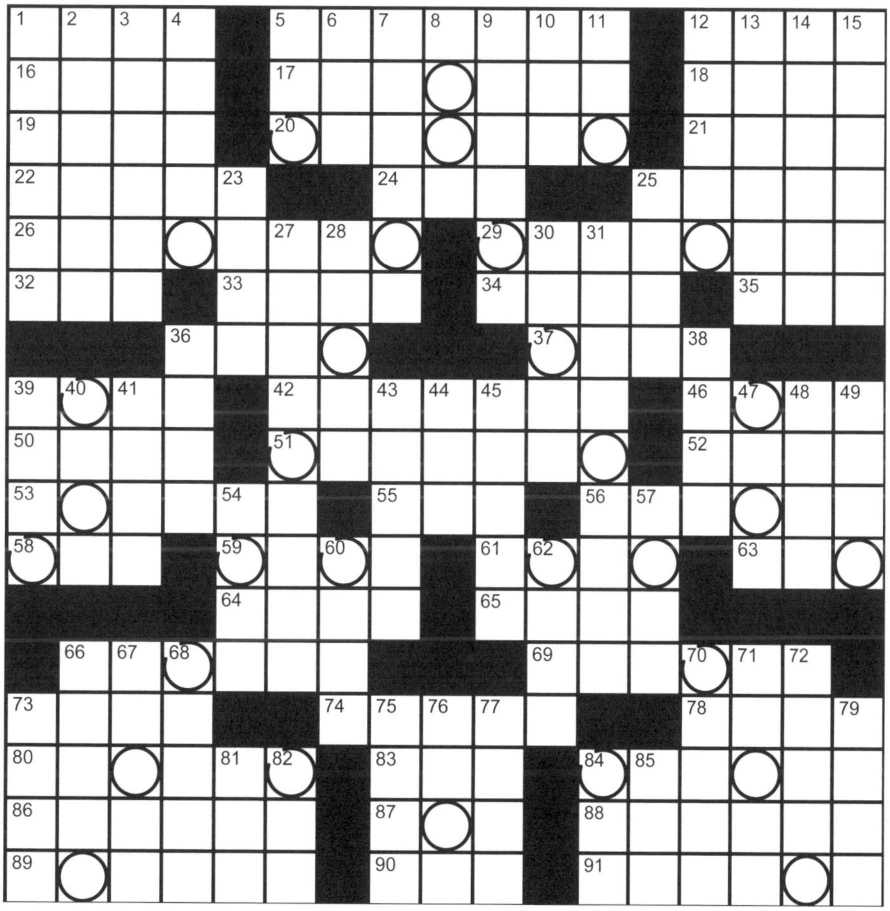
1 2 3 4 5 6 7 8 9 10 11 12 13 14 15
16 17 18
19 20 21
22 23 24 25
26 27 28 29 30 31
32 33 34 35
36 37 38
39 40 41 42 43 44 45 46 47 48 49
50 51 52
53 54 55 56 57
58 59 60 61 62 63
64 65
66 67 68 69 70 71 72
73 74 75 76 77 78 79
80 81 82 83 84 85
86 87 88
89 90 91

USHERING IN THE DAWN

CONCLUDING THOUGHT FROM EMMA GOLDMAN

ACROSS

1 GPA, GDP, and RBI
6 Deck attraction
12 6-7, in bowling
17 Pre-Soviet cooperative
18 Parmesan alternative
19 Solo
20 Quote, part 1
23 Be a scrub
24 Anglo folks
25 Quote, part 2
30 Showing off at a wine-tasting, say
31 Breathing moments
36 Bancroft played her in 1977's *Golda*
37 Afrocentric believer
42 Quote, part 3
47 His story was Disney-fied in 1992
48 Attractive apparel
49 Polish river that anagrams to a seabird
50 "Chill!"
55 Cee follower, for an academic?
56 Card in Monopoly
58 "Over the Rainbow" song form
59 Iraq War worries: Abbr.

60 With 71-Across, source of the quote
67 Apple Pencil, e.g.
68 Honeydew of The Muppets
71 See 60-Across
77 Smooth transition
80 Garlicky sauces
81 Yogurt-and-cucumber side dish
82 Kensington Park residents
83 Strossen, ACLU president 1991–2008
84 Insurance co. with a duck logo
85 Using few words
86 Window accents
87 Canada fowl

DOWN

1 Comic ___
2 Pledge of fidelity
3 Many lobbies
4 Social media influencers, often
5 Satisfy, as a thirst
6 Pick up the tempo
7 Bear in the Cantabrian Mountains
8 Twitch
9 ___ chi chuan (exercise regimen)

10 Athens sch.
11 Ray of *The Wizard of Oz*
12 South Asian title during the Raj
13 Town near Dallas
14 Amusing vowel sound?
15 Bit of bullion
16 Golfer's pocketful, possibly
21 WCs
22 Blues guitarist Robert
26 Marinara tomatoes
27 For example, Bo Darville in *Smokey and the Bandit*
28 Heidi Schreck won it for *What the Constitution Means to Me*
29 Griffin who created *Jeopardy!*
31 Kigali location
32 Fisher of fasion, et al.
33 Gawk
34 Deg. awarded the Scarecrow
35 Lays a lawn
37 Wrack partner
38 Czech's bankomat: Abbr.
39 Pasta strainer
40 Built
41 Contributes to the pot
43 Quick turnaround for a driver?

44 It's used in Minecraft
45 ___ Grande Mine in Arizona
46 Firm area?
51 Prof.'s aides
52 Take it on the ___
53 Monogram for the author of *Charlotte's Web*: inits.
54 Telegrapher's syllable
57 Beta tests, essentially
59 "No need to fear."
61 Star of *Hold the Sunset* and *Fawlty Towers*
62 Mount ___, one of the Five Great Mountains of China
63 Manhattan, for example
64 Demeans
65 Winery cask
66 How RuPaul performs
69 Option via irs.gov
70 ___ good (less satisfying)
72 Fabulist, in a way
73 "There is no try." speaker
74 Fall on the ice
75 Fork feature
76 Run competitively
77 Concorde, for one
78 Lady of the lea
79 Fish related to the bowfin

CONSTRUCTOR'S NOTES

Use this key as a guide to the level of challenge presented by each puzzle:

SLIGHT CHALLENGE ⚐

MODERATE CHALLENGE ⚐⚐

SUBSTANTIAL CHALLENGE ⚐⚐⚐

GENERAL STRIKE ⚐

Because the theme for this puzzle initiated the entire project, it is quite fitting for it to serve as the opening puzzle of the book. The wordplay employed follows from the title, so it should be relatively easy to solve once you supply the missing pieces.

INTERSECTIONALITY ⚐

The concept of intersectionality, advanced by the Combahee River Collective and by Kimberlé Crenshaw, is now a staple of radical theory and practice. Entries in the grid not only contain, but also illustrate, elements of such intersections.

HAVEN ⚐⚐

The puzzle contains a quotation that is relatively easy to parse and solve, but there is a bonus element that adds additional difficulty. The shaded squares illustrate the concept at the heart of the puzzle, along with what is known as a Schrödinger entry in which the clue and the solution work with more than one correct answer.

HAYMARKET ⚐⚐

The Haymarket Affair is notable in the history of anarchism and organized labor in the United States. This straightforward tribute puzzle identifies the martyrs and includes related material. Not all the facts are common knowledge, which adds some difficulty to the solve. Feel free to look up those that are unfamiliar. Use this opportunity to learn more about history.

AFFINITY GROUP ⚐

Affinity groups have long been a primary way for anarchists to organize. Spanish anarchists in the early twentieth century employed them, as have radical movements in the United States and elsewhere since the 1960s. This puzzle highlights the importance of elective affinities through a crossword convention—theme entries that use words having something in common.

DIRECT ACTION

Here is a puzzle built around an apt quotation from a similarly titled book by the phenomenal writer and activist identified at 81-Across. The quotation's individual entries are not divided at punctuation indicators, so it may be difficult to parse at first. Read as a whole, though, it clearly and ably defines the concept of direct action. Sadly, some three months after this puzzle was created, anarchists and other radicals had to mourn the writer's sudden passing. Rest in Power, comrade.

WHY THE BLACK FLAG?

The color symbolism used here is drawn from the similarly titled essay printed in Howard J. Ehrlich, ed., *Reinventing Anarchy, Again.* Each theme entry captures one of the possible symbolic meanings of the color black. A small touch of grid art here provides a bonus.

MUTUAL AID

The before-and-after theme here underscores the "mutual" aspect of mutual aid.

CAPITALIST PYRAMID

Although somewhat unfamiliar, the theme entries come from an illustration in the *Industrial Worker* (1911) that is often reproduced (facing). Search for it on the Internet and learn more about its provenance.

CIVILIZATION AND ITS DISCONTENTS

The title is taken from a famous work by Sigmund Freud. The straightforward theme entries do not reflect Freud, but rather refer to concerns advanced by anarcho-primitivists and other anti-civilization activists.

PREFIGURATIVE POLITICS

Prefigurative politics is a mode of organization and action that anticipates elements of the future society that one envisions. It embodies a unity of means and ends reflected in this puzzle's theme entries.

ANTI-HIERARCHY

Opposition to hierarchical social arrangements is an important concept in anarchist thought. (For more on this idea, see Randall Amster's contribution to *Anarchism: A Conceptual Approach*, edited by Benjamin Franks, Nathan Jun, and Leonard Williams.) This puzzle uses a standard crossword mechanism to express that opposition.

ANOTHER WORLD IS POSSIBLE

As the title indicates, this puzzle was inspired by a slogan associated with the anti- or alter-globalization movement. Take the phrase somewhat literally to reimagine our condition or, at least, to figure out the wordplay used here.

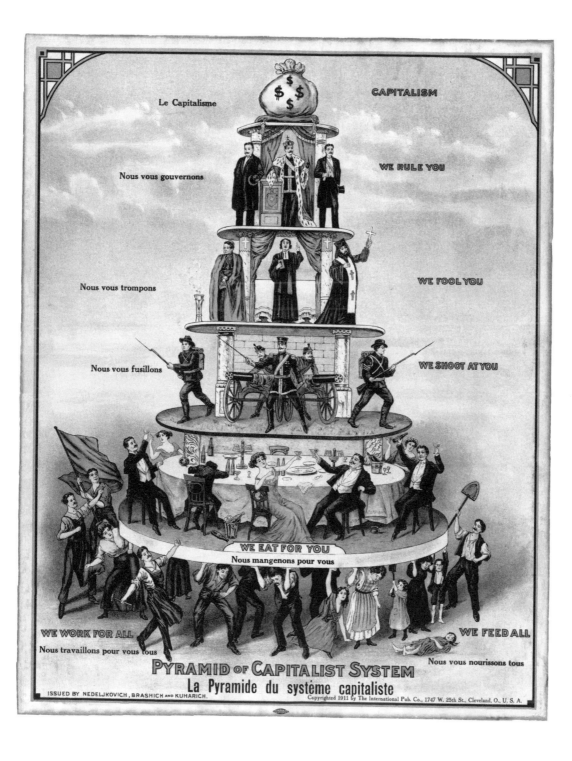

FROM MARGIN TO CENTER

The puzzle takes its title from one of the many instructive and classic works by bell hooks. The theme entries reference the titles of other classics in the feminist canon.

SMASHY SMASHY

As the Bakunin quote suggests, you will need to engage metaphorically in both passions (creation and destruction) to solve this challenging puzzle.

ANARCHO-SYNDICALISM

Entries related to the theory and practice of anarcho-syndicalism are featured here and clued in a straightforward manner.

LEADERLESS RESISTANCE

Leaderless resistance is a longstanding organizational strategy for radical movements. Use a literal understanding of the term to solve each part of the theme entries in this puzzle.

VISION FOR BLACK LIVES

The grid's theme entries highlight aspects of the significant and detailed policy agenda advanced by the Movement for Black Lives.

GENDER TROUBLE

Quite obviously, this puzzle was inspired by the title of Judith Butler's famous book. The focus here is not on her thesis that gender is performative, but on the idea that its various aspects are not as stable as we think they are—that is, we can regard gender as "troubled." Understanding this puzzle depends on knowing that the word "troubled" can signal the need to anagram words in cryptic crossword clues.

ABC

This puzzle's straightforward theme is built around a bit of grid art and the long entry at 87-Across. The organization has been assisting comrades in struggle for many decades.

WITH THE WOBBLIES

Theme entries riff on the aim of creating "one big union" as advocated by the Industrial Workers of the World. The puzzle contains a couple of bonus nods to the IWW as well.

FREE WOMEN / MUJERES LIBRES

The puzzle references several prominent women in the anarchist movement. Two of the women name-checked in the puzzle were co-founders of *Mujeres Libres,* an anarchist women's organization that operated in Spain during the late 1930s.

A MEDITATION ON THE STATE

This puzzle is built around a famous quotation from Mikhail Bakunin's *Statism and Anarchy* (1873).

SONGS OF THE WILD

References to rock songs are featured in this puzzle that riffs on the notion of the wild prominent in anti-civilizational thought and practice.

ABOLITIONIST SLOGANS

The theme entries are phrases involving institutions or practices that anarchists would like to abolish. These phrases are reimagined as bases for new-fangled political slogans.

COMPANION PLANTING

The theme here draws upon and illustrates a key principle of permaculture. Solving help can be found in the title, the hint, and the context of the puzzle.

SEEDS BENEATH THE SNOW

The puzzle's descriptive note references to the IWW-related aim of "building a new world in the shell of the old." To parse the puzzle's theme entries correctly, take this idea quite literally.

DELEGATES' MEETING

Filling the grid itself should be relatively easy but grasping the theme may prove more difficult. That additional level of difficulty might even earn the puzzle an extra ▶. Shaded and circled squares have been added to help one imagine the process involved in the meetings of delegates from represented groups.

DECLARATION OF A FREETHINKER

Voltairine de Cleyre was a notable individualist anarchist or freethinker. The focus of the puzzle is a remark she made in the context of distinguishing between rights and privileges in her essay on "The Economic Tendency of Freethought." The quotation may be hard to parse because of its nineteenth-century syntax. Here are some hints: After starting with 17-Across, insert a comma after 22-Across. A semicolon should follow 46-Across. You should insert another comma after 75-Across, before concluding with 82-Across.

#SAYTHEIRNAMES

Exactly. Do so while you solve. Do so after you finish.

SOCIAL RELATIONSHIPS

The puzzle takes ordinary phrases and reinterprets them as commentaries on social groups.

DESTROYING DOMINATION

Opposition to systems of domination is a central tenet of anarchist theory and practice. Clues for the theme entries initially focus on a form of domination that has already been "destroyed," that is, restructured or modified. The parenthetical element of the clue alludes to the unreconstructed version.

NOISE DEMO

Although they originated elsewhere, noise demonstrations have been used in the US. Most commonly, they have been employed in prisoner support and prison abolition contexts. As a nod to their South American origins, I included a somewhat obscure term at 62-Across.

POSTANARCHISM

One of the most influential theoretical books in the last decade or so has been *The Politics of Postanarchism* by Saul Newman. This puzzle highlights some of the ideas expressed in that work.

RECOGNITION

Several professional sports teams have long had problematic nicknames. For a few of them, this puzzle seeks to extend recognition to various tribes, based on the lands for which they traditionally provided stewardship. Fortunately, some of the teams mentioned already have begun the process of changing their nicknames. May more teams at all levels do so.

ON FERALITY

Ferality is a concept employed by people associated with several contemporary anarchist tendencies. (To begin exploring the concept, see Feral Faun, *Feral Revolution and Other Essays*.) For green anarchists and anarcho-primitivists, ferality is related to the concept of rewilding—an idea that expresses a resistance to domestication. Among post-leftist and insurrectionary tendencies, being wild or feral stresses the notion that people should essentially be ungovernable, poised to resist power and domination in all its manifestations. The wordplay in this puzzle focuses on notions of the "feral."

PREFIGURATION

If prefigurative politics anticipates elements of the new world that one envisions, this puzzle involves some literal foreshadowing of that future. (Each adjective offers an apt description of the noun it modifies.)

RECLAIM THE STREETS ▰▰

Reclaim the Streets is a direct-action organization that was originally formed in London in 1991. Since then, the idea of reclaiming the streets for people rather than automobiles has been a significant tactic used in the context of various actions and movements. Using a crossword-based understanding of "reclaiming" (that is, embracing or including), each theme entry reclaims a street—but with a linguistic twist.

STRATEGIC DISRUPTION ▰▰

The title of this puzzle reflects one aim of radical political action. Rather than employ a straightforward presentation, though, the arrangement of theme entries (see the starred clues) in the grid should illustrate the theme itself.

GRAFFITI ▰▰

The demonstrations and uprisings in France during May 1968 produced marvelous examples of radical graffiti. Much like Zen koans, the specific sayings or slogans are subject to multiple, if not contradictory, interpretations. The ones embedded in the grid are among my favorites, drawn from what seems to be a comprehensive list published in the *Situationist International Anthology*, Revised and Expanded Edition, edited by Ken Knabb.

DEMOCRACY IN THE WORKPLACE ▰▰

Workplace democracy has long been an aim of syndicalists and other radicals. In this puzzle, democracy (understood in a particular way) becomes disruptive of three workplaces (though not necessarily representative ones).

TRANSGRESSING BOUNDARIES ▰▰▰

This challenging puzzle plays with the idea of undermining national boundaries. No documentation is required to cross the boundaries, but crossing can only happen in certain areas (as if they were mountain gaps, fordable rivers, tunnels, et cetera).

POST-ANARCHIST TENDENCIES ▰

This one involves rather standard wordplay, hinted at by the description. Add "anarchist" to the "end" of the two-word phrases. The descriptive hint should help, but in case it does not, think about this puzzle as an exercise in word association.

SOCIAL ECOLOGY ▰▰

This large puzzle employs some of the key concepts in social ecology. Theme entry clues are suggestive rather than straightforward, which should add a little challenge.

ESSENTIAL EGOISM ⮞⮞

The philosophy of Max Stirner, one of the Young Hegelians in the nineteenth century, has seen a resurgence of popularity among some groups of anarchists in recent years. His philosophical egoism, like that of Nietzsche, reflects an individualism that appeals to the general spirit of rebellion that animates anarchist thought. Stirner has been influential among activists and writers regarded as individualist anarchists, post-left anarchists, or post-anarchists. Insert a comma before the square at 30-Down to parse the featured quotation from Stirner's *The Ego and Its Own* (Second Part, Chapter I).

PERMACULTURE ⮞⮞

Some of the principles of permaculture, as a sustainable approach to gardening and design, are profiled here.

TRANSVALUATION OF VALUES ⮞⮞

Theme entries are clued as if they have been trans-valued. In other words, grasping the solution is in the stars.

INTEGRATED LABOR ⮞⮞

This a tribute puzzle to a work by 36-Across. See the ends of the theme entries (29-, 45-, and 17- & 60-Across) for the book title.

DESTABILIZING HIERARCHIES ⮞⮞⮞

This puzzle may be the most challenging of all. Given the puzzle's focus on hierarchies, the theme entries are arranged vertically. Each one is "destabilized" in a different way, as noted in the respective clue. A solver thus needs to get an answer and then modify it according to the parenthetical instruction. (One additional element may give the puzzle an extra level of difficulty: There is a theme answer that contains a "rebus" square that encompasses two letters. It signifies one letter in the down entry and a different letter in the across entry.)

TAG, YOU'RE IT! ⮞⮞

The correct solution to this puzzle lets you connect the "dots" (similar letters in circles) to reproduce a well-known graffiti tag.

USHERING IN THE DAWN ⮞⮞

I was happy to fit both an Emma Goldman quotation and its source into this puzzle. The grid uses left-right symmetry, so it may appear a little strange initially. Fun Fact: My first anarchist-related puzzle was entitled "Red Emma," which appeared in *The Penguin Classics Crossword Puzzles*, edited by Ben Tausig. Coincidentally, it also involved a quotation from Goldman's work.

Grid 1 (top-left)

```
T I P J A R . A S S T . B P S
Y O U A R E . T A R O . O A T
P U B L I C R A D I O . F L O
E S S . . E A R . . O F F E R
. . H O S P I T A L R O O M .
H A B E A S . . R I D E . . .
I C E R S . A L U M . E S P O
P R A C T I C E S E S S I O N
S O T U . M C A T . H O T E L
. . L A D E . . F E I S T Y .
A S S E M B L Y H A L L . . .
N O T S O . . O U T . I L O .
D R E . S T O R E C R E D I T
R E A . O K O K . A B S E N T
E L K . Z O N E . T I E S T O
```

Grid 2 (top-right)

```
T R A P . C L A P . S E D A N
W A L L . E I R E . P A I N E
I C E E . D E E T . E R A S E
S E X A G E N A R I A N S . .
T R I T E . . O C K . P V C .
S S E . N A M E L Y . Z O E Y
. . A T H O S . M O R E S . .
N E O C L A S S I C A L A R T
E M P T Y . . E A S Y A . . .
A M E S . H E X N U T . C T A
T A N . W E S . . A D L E R .
. P R I N C E S S G R A C E .
S A L O N . A P O P . I S A N
I R A T E . P I S A . E S T A
D E N I S . E C O N . D Y E S
```

Grid 3 (bottom-left)

```
P E S C A . R A G E . C A R B
E L L E S . E L I A . A G E E
L O A T H . C E R T I T U D E
L I B E R A T E D A R E A O F
. . R A D O . S M A . . . . .
P A J A M A . . E N T I R E .
I C E . . U N T P A I N T E D
L A N D . S T A H L . T I M E
O R G A N I Z E D . N I N . .
T E A P O T . . E C L A T S .
. . R U E . I R A E . . . . .
. O R I M A G I N A T I O N .
C R O S S T A L K . T L A I B
S E M I . E L S E . L A T T E
T O P S . D E A D . E S S A Y
```

Grid 4 (bottom-right)

```
A I S H A . S C H W A B . A L E E
S T E A L . T R O I K A . S I G N
E I G H T H O U R D A Y . S N A G
A S A . H E L E N E . A N G L E
. . P E T A . N D A S . G E L .
H U R R A H F O R . E C H O . .
A P O C . . N E W A T . R S V P
R H O . A D O L P H F I S C H E R
D I M . P O P O . O T O E . O N O
A L B E R T P A R S O N S . R U T
S L A W . C O N D O . A T E E .
. . E R O S . A N A R C H I S M
S S N . A M E S . M O O S . . .
P I E T Y . T E N D T O . P U P
I D E E . M A R S E I L L A I S E
E L B A . I G U A N A . I B S E N
S E E K . S A M U E L . T V A D S
```

Puzzle 1 (top-left)

```
TIFF  CREAMPIE  UTE
ARLO  HARDTACK  SAS
ROOMMATEAGREEMENT
ONPOINT  MER  USNA
     STEP    UPTOIT
FAMILYRESEMBLANCE
OHARA   NEWMOON
GETRICH  LAVA  TYRE
GMT  DEAN  NITE  AAS
YSER  NYSE  ISLANDS
   ESTEEMS   ERNIE
NETWORKCONNECTION
EXHALE    LILT
PURR   CUI  ENROLLS
ALUMNIASSOCIATION
LTS  NORSEMEN  INCA
ISH  ESPRESSO  SKIP
```

Puzzle 2 (top-right)

```
AMASS  FIASCO  AARP
CASCO  ISINON  RIAA
INSOFARASONE  GRPS
DEARTH  AHOT  PUPAS
STYE  ISCAPABLEONE
    RASA   CEE  RUR
OIL  MENU  ATLANTIS
PROCEEDSAS  ADE
SAGE  PARKS   ALAS
    ROZ  IFTHESTATE
SEANPENN  OEDS  MMA
EXT  IRE   DINE
DOESNOTEXIST  NATS
ATALE  GATO  OLDPRO
RITA  DAVIDGRAEBER
ICON  AMELIE  SAINT
SANG  RESECT  TROTS
```

Puzzle 3 (bottom-left)

```
SNAFU  IDOS   PLATO
RUBIK  ROUTE  OILER
AMENU  OOZED  OMANI
   ALONZOMOURNING
   LEROI    PHI
DOUBLENEGATION
ERNIE   ONE  UGLIS
NERD  GROANERS  ACE
ILE  FREELANCE  DEL
ESS  RETSINAS  VIAL
SETAE  ATE    BINGE
   REPRESSEDANGER
   MTA   ONRYE
AMERICANBEAUTY
SIDEB  LILAC  RASTA
IRISE  BLEST  ERRED
AVETT   EDYS  EDITS
```

Puzzle 4 (bottom-right)

```
SITS  PSALM  LEHI
MAHI  ALGIA  AXON
OMEN  DEALWITHIT
LIFESUPPORTHOSE
DSO  KATE   SERIN
EARLY    ODE  TNT
RICO  STABILE
  DEBTRELIEFMAP
   ORANGES  TNUT
FOR  OST   ASANA
ALEAP   OMAR  LIL
KITCHENHELPDESK
IVORYCOAST  OCHS
NILE  HORSE  STET
GADS  ONAIR  ESSO
```

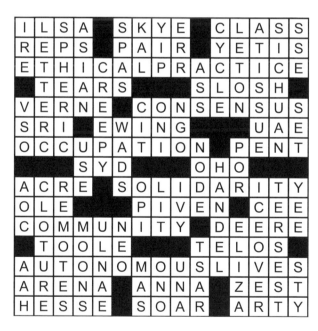

P	I	C	A	■	S	L	O	B	■	N	O	H	O	■	N	O	A	H
A	C	U	P	■	E	A	S	Y	■	S	W	A	N	■	E	B	R	O
W	E	R	U	L	E	Y	O	U	■	F	I	L	E	C	L	E	R	K
P	D	T	■	I	M	S	■	■	■	W	E	F	O	O	L	Y	O	U
A	T	E	A	M	S	■	L	A	G	■	■	A	F	R	■	S	W	M
W	E	S	H	O	O	T	A	T	Y	O	U	■	F	F	A	■	■	■
S	A	T	E	■	■	I	M	E	M	I	N	E	■	U	R	S	U	S
■	■	■	A	K	I	M	B	O	■	L	O	T	S	■	I	T	H	E
C	A	R	D	I	B	■	D	U	E	■	■	S	T	C	L	O	U	D
A	B	A	■	W	E	E	A	T	F	O	R	Y	O	U	■	I	R	A
P	O	N	T	I	A	C	■	■	T	R	E	■	C	T	S	C	A	N
R	U	D	E	■	M	I	T	T	■	A	W	A	K	E	N	■	■	■
A	T	O	M	S	■	G	R	O	T	T	O	S	■	■	A	L	I	A
■	■	■	P	A	M	■	W	E	W	O	R	K	F	O	R	A	L	L
O	R	I	■	L	A	P	■	■	O	R	D	■	A	G	E	O	L	D
W	E	F	E	E	D	A	L	L	■	■	■	L	T	R	■	T	E	E
L	A	N	D	S	L	I	D	E	■	P	E	A	C	E	S	I	G	N
E	T	O	N	■	I	N	R	E	■	O	K	R	A	■	B	A	I	T
T	A	T	A	■	B	E	S	S	■	P	E	S	T	■	A	N	T	E

A	C	H	E	■	C	M	I	I	■	G	O	S	S	I	P	S
B	R	O	A	D	B	A	N	D	■	O	P	E	N	S	E	A
C	O	M	M	O	D	I	T	Y	■	D	E	P	O	S	E	R
S	W	E	E	T	■	A	R	L	E	S	■	T	R	U	R	O
■	■	■	S	E	C	■	A	L	I	E	N	A	T	I	O	N
T	E	A	■	R	O	O	■	■	R	N	A	■	S	N	U	G
I	N	D	U	S	T	R	Y	■	E	D	G	E	■	G	T	S
M	O	H	S	■	■	B	E	D	■	■	A	P	T	■	■	■
■	■	D	O	M	E	S	T	I	C	A	T	I	O	N	■	■
■	■	■	C	A	R	■	■	M	E	W	■	■	F	E	A	R
C	C	S	■	C	A	V	S	■	L	A	N	G	U	A	G	E
I	L	E	T	■	T	A	T	■	■	Y	E	A	■	T	O	M
T	E	C	H	N	O	L	O	G	Y	■	B	L	T	■	■	■
R	A	R	E	E	■	J	A	C	O	B	■	P	O	R	T	S
O	N	E	L	O	V	E	■	H	I	E	R	A	R	C	H	Y
E	S	T	O	N	I	A	■	A	N	T	E	L	O	P	E	S
N	E	S	T	S	I	N	■	T	K	O	D	■	S	T	E	T

I	L	S	A	■	S	K	Y	E	■	C	L	A	S	S
R	E	P	S	■	P	A	I	R	■	Y	E	T	I	S
E	T	H	I	C	A	L	P	R	A	C	T	I	C	E
■	T	E	A	R	S	■	■	■	S	L	O	S	H	■
V	E	R	N	E	■	C	O	N	S	E	N	S	U	S
S	R	I	■	E	W	I	N	G	■	■	■	U	A	E
O	C	C	U	P	A	T	I	O	N	■	P	E	N	T
■	■	■	S	Y	D	■	■	■	O	H	O	■	■	■
A	C	R	E	■	S	O	L	I	D	A	R	I	T	Y
O	L	E	■	■	■	P	I	V	E	N	■	C	E	E
C	O	M	M	U	N	I	T	Y	■	D	E	E	R	E
■	T	O	O	L	E	■	■	■	T	E	L	O	S	■
A	U	T	O	N	O	M	O	U	S	L	I	V	E	S
A	R	E	N	A	■	A	N	N	A	■	Z	E	S	T
H	E	S	S	E	■	S	O	A	R	■	A	R	T	Y

A	R	C	S	■	E	M	E	R	I	T	I	■	C	A	S	T
N	E	H	I	■	H	A	T	E	S	O	N	■	O	P	I	E
G	M	A	N	■	R	I	C	H	T	E	R	■	R	P	M	S
■	■	L	E	V	E	L	H	E	A	D	E	D	N	E	S	S
U	T	I	C	A	■	■	I	A	N	■	■	R	I	A	■	■
R	E	C	U	M	B	E	N	T	B	I	C	Y	C	L	E	■
B	E	E	R	P	O	N	G	■	U	R	L	■	E	S	S	O
■	■	■	V	I	L	A	S	■	L	E	A	D	■	T	P	K
H	E	T	E	R	O	■	■	■	■	■	M	A	S	O	N	S
A	N	I	■	E	T	C	H	■	A	V	A	S	T	■	■	■
M	U	T	T	■	I	P	A	■	W	I	T	H	E	R	E	D
■	F	L	A	T	E	A	R	T	H	S	O	C	I	E	T	Y
■	■	E	R	A	■	■	D	I	E	■	■	A	N	T	E	S
H	O	R	I	Z	O	N	T	A	L	M	A	M	B	O	■	■
A	S	O	F	■	S	C	A	R	L	E	T	■	E	T	A	L
H	A	L	F	■	H	O	S	A	N	N	A	■	C	A	G	E
A	Y	E	S	■	A	S	K	S	O	U	T	■	K	L	E	E

Puzzle 1 (top-left)

```
B B C   S T E P S   P A I D
A O R B   I A L S O   H U L U
Y O U R O C K M Y P L A N E T
S T E A D I E S     A R T S Y
    H O L M   S O D A
  J I M M Y E A T G L O B E
L A S S     S U R E H A N D
A N I   A B O D E   B U N
S E A W A T E R   N A R C
  T H E L O S T S P H E R E
    I O N S   C R E W
S N A R F   W H E R E A M I
D E A D T O T H E C O S M O S
A U R A   M I A M I   T O R I
K E E L   G A T E S   N E S
```

Puzzle 2 (top-right)

```
F O S S E   C A T S A T   P O M E L O S
M O N I E S   A S E A S Y   R A I M E N T
A S L E E P   S I S T E R O U T S I D E R
C S I S   E T A L I A   I D E S   B R A
A I N T I A W O M A N   L E N   H U E S
O L E A N D E R   A M E N   T A L E S
    L A S   G E N D E R T R O U B L E
S C A R A B   A S A N A S   O P T
T A L O N   A M I S T A D   C M I   P C T
A V I N D I C A T I O N   O R A C U L A R
R I G A   N E T S   U D O N   D I V E
C A N N A B I S   T H E S E C O N D S E X
H R S   D E T   R O A R E R S   O E S T E
    O A T   L E S T A T   B E R E T S
S C U M M A N I F E S T O   M A V
N O N O S   O K I E   O B R I G A D O
O N T O   S T E   B O R D E R L A N D S
W V A   T O E S   L A D I E S   S U R A
S E X U A L P O L I T I C S   A C T B I G
I N E R T I A   E C O L E S   T H R I V E
N E D L U D D   G E N E R A   M O O S E
```

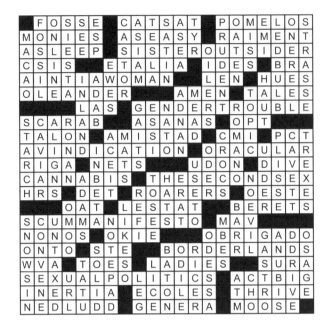

Puzzle 3 (bottom-left)

```
S I M   C U S P   W I S H E S
O D E   A S H E   A G L E T S
F O L D T E E S   I N A R O W
T I D E S   B O S T O N
O D E A   E A S T E R T A L E
N O D D E D   E R E   W O N
    E E Y O R E   W O O S
  L O N G S H I P P S A L M
B A U D   L O S I N G
A M S   T I O   C L E R K S
R E T R O F O N T S   G A I T
    H O O K A H   S A R E E
S T J O H N   T O R Y P E R P
T V I D O L   A S I S   S A O
S A F E T Y   L E F T   T N N
```

Puzzle 4 (bottom-right)

```
Z A P P A   S T A T E D   C H O W
E P E E S   D E N A L I   H A R I
D I R E C T A C T I O N   A W E D
    P I N K   P A S S A G E
O P T S I N   F E D E R A T I O N
C U E   A I D E   V E I N S
C L A S S S T R U G G L E
A L T R U I S M   S O O   D A Y O
M A R T I N I   S N E E R A T
S T O A   C G T   D O G P A R K S
  G E N E R A L S T R I K E
S A G A L   R E M O   B E G
T R A D E U N I O N   N O T A R O
R E L I E V E   B O B A
O N E D   R U D O L F R O C K E R
D A N A   A R A B I A   E K I N G
E S A S   Y O D E L S   S Y N C S
```

Grid 1 (top-left)

S	I	M	B	A	■	B	L	A	H	■	D	I	N	G
H	O	A	R	D	■	E	I	N	E	■	A	C	A	I
O	N	V	I	O	L	E	N	T	R	O	T	E	S	T
E	S	S	E	N	E	■	C	I	A	B	A	T	T	A
■	■	■	F	A	S	T	■	■	L	O	S	■	■	■
I	V	I	L	I	S	O	B	E	D	I	E	N	C	E
D	E	N	Y	■	S	L	A	V	■	S	T	E	A	L
I	D	S	■	H	O	T	S	E	A	T	■	G	M	O
N	I	E	C	E	■	E	I	N	S	■	A	R	E	A
A	C	T	O	R	Y	C	C	U	P	A	T	I	O	N
■	■	■	U	M	A	■	■	P	I	L	E	■	■	■
C	O	L	L	A	P	S	E	■	R	I	A	L	T	O
R	M	E	D	N	S	U	R	R	E	C	T	I	O	N
A	N	O	N	■	A	L	I	I	■	I	O	N	I	C
M	I	N	T	■	T	A	C	O	■	A	N	K	L	E

Grid 2 (top-right)

H	E	M	P	■	T	O	S	C	A	■	C	O	N	S
O	P	P	O	■	O	S	C	A	R	■	A	B	U	T
T	E	A	L	■	P	H	A	R	M	■	F	O	I	A
H	E	A	L	T	H	A	N	D	S	A	F	E	T	Y
■	■	■	O	V	A	■	I	O	N	E	■	■	■	■
R	E	D	I	S	T	R	I	B	U	T	I	O	N	■
A	Q	I	■	S	I	S	■	T	E	N	N	I	S	■
P	U	P	I	L	■	G	A	G	■	D	E	L	T	A
A	I	S	L	E	S	■	A	P	U	■	O	R	D	■
■	P	O	L	I	T	I	C	A	L	P	O	W	E	R
■	■	U	L	A	N	■	■	U	S	C	■	■	■	■
L	A	W	S	A	N	D	P	O	L	I	C	I	E	S
O	H	H	I	■	C	I	A	R	A	■	U	N	D	O
O	M	O	O	■	E	G	R	E	T	■	P	G	D	N
M	E	A	N	■	S	O	M	M	E	■	Y	E	A	S

Grid 3 (bottom-left)

A	B	C	S	■	C	A	S	H	■	C	O	T	T	A
B	L	O	C	■	A	L	P	E	■	A	P	E	A	R
L	E	A	H	■	T	E	R	N	■	R	E	L	I	C
Y	U	L	E	T	A	X	I	S	I	D	L	E	■	■
■	■	M	A	C	■	G	O	B	I	■	H	I	C	■
C	A	K	E	P	O	P	■	N	O	B	U	E	N	O
O	N	E	■	I	M	H	O	■	■	H	A	H	A	■
A	N	Y	I	N	B	O	R	N	R	E	F	L	E	X
R	U	L	E	■	■	S	H	A	Q	■	T	R	E	■
S	A	I	D	I	D	O	■	S	L	U	S	H	E	D
E	L	M	■	D	O	U	R	■	L	I	T	■	■	■
■	■	E	D	I	T	T	I	N	Y	P	O	E	M	S
G	O	P	R	O	■	B	N	A	I	■	P	R	E	P
T	A	I	N	T	■	I	S	A	N	■	I	O	T	A
O	R	E	O	S	■	D	E	N	G	■	T	S	A	R

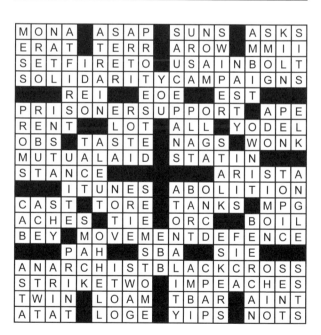

Grid 4 (bottom-right)

M	O	N	A	■	A	S	A	P	■	S	U	N	S	■	A	S	K	S
E	R	A	T	■	T	E	R	R	■	A	R	O	W	■	M	M	I	I
S	E	T	F	I	R	E	T	O	■	U	S	A	I	N	B	O	L	T
S	O	L	I	D	A	R	I	T	Y	C	A	M	P	A	I	G	N	S
■	■	R	E	I	■	■	E	O	E	■	■	E	S	T	■	■	■	■
P	R	I	S	O	N	E	R	S	U	P	P	O	R	T	■	A	P	E
R	E	N	T	■	■	L	O	T	■	A	L	L	■	Y	O	D	E	L
O	B	S	■	T	A	S	T	E	■	N	A	G	S	■	W	O	N	K
M	U	T	U	A	L	A	I	D	■	S	T	A	T	I	N	■	■	■
S	T	A	N	C	E	■	■	■	■	■	A	R	I	S	T	A	■	■
■	■	I	T	U	N	E	S	■	A	B	O	L	I	T	I	O	N	■
C	A	S	T	■	T	O	R	E	■	T	A	N	K	S	■	M	P	G
A	C	H	E	S	■	T	I	E	■	O	R	C	■	B	O	I	L	■
B	E	Y	■	M	O	V	E	M	E	N	T	D	E	F	E	N	C	E
■	■	■	P	A	H	■	■	S	B	A	■	S	I	E	■	■	■	■
A	N	A	R	C	H	I	S	T	B	L	A	C	K	C	R	O	S	S
S	T	R	I	K	E	T	W	O	■	I	M	P	E	A	C	H	E	S
T	W	I	N	■	L	O	A	M	■	T	B	A	R	■	A	I	N	T
A	T	A	T	■	L	O	G	E	■	Y	I	P	S	■	N	O	T	S

Puzzle 1 (top-left)

```
C A M U S . . P E A R L E . . S K A
A G A S P . . S A N D B A R . O R C
F A S H I O N P O L I C E . . L I T
. . . E R O I C A . . . D I S .
. M A S L O W S H I E R A R C H Y
A I M E . N I T . L O V E I N S
R A I N S O N . V A L L I . T A L
M O N T Y . C A S E L A W .
. W O R L D D O M I N A T I O N
. . A L O A D O F . . O L D I E
A M O . A R B Y S . C A R D I F F
B A B Y B I B . A R S . E S T S
C H E M I C A L P R O P E R T Y
. A L A . . E A R W I G
A L I . R E F E R E N C E W O R K
M I S . A G E L E S S . S T I N E
Y A K . M O Z A R T . T O D A Y
```

Puzzle 2 (top-right)

```
B O M E R . D E L I . S H A W
S A N A A . R E I N . P A S A
S H O R T C A K E S . O I L S
. U P P E R M A N H A T T A N
. . I D A . A N O I N T
P A P E R M A T E P E N
E P I C . S C O N E S . J A I
T O T E M . U N A . T B A L L
S P Y . A S T E R S . I D O L
. H Y P E R M A R K E T S
I T S Y O U . T A E
S U P E R M A R I O B R O S
O P E N . O N I O N B A G E L
L A N A . N O O N . I C E R S
A C T S . E N T S . S K E E T
```

Puzzle 3 (bottom-left)

```
G A P S . B A A . D O H A . P K G
U C L A . A D E . E D E N . R O O
A T O M I Z E R . N E E D I E S T
C A P I T A (S)(O)(C)(I) A L I S M
. O A T B A R . S E R I A L
S E R F (F)(R)(E)(E) D O M . E G O
W H A R F S . E A T C R O W
F U B U . S E A O T T E R
D O M I N (L)(I)(B)(E)(R) A T I O N
. P L E A S E D O . S T O W
P E N S E E S . I M P I S H
A D A . H I E R (A) N A R C H Y
R U S S I A . N E A R E D
C E N T R (F)(E)(D)(E)(R) A L I S M
S W E E T T E A . N O T T O D A Y
T O N . R E A M . E L I . E E L S
Y E T . O N L Y . R E A . W A T T
```

Puzzle 4 (bottom-right)

```
S E A D O O . W R I T H E S
O R G A N D Y . R E F O R G E
O N (E) R O O M . S P I E (S) O N
T E N (K) . R C S . A D (P)
. S T L (O) . A I R C (O) O L E D
. Y U (P) . L E (K) . K A L E
S W F . N O (S)(E) E . A E R I E
C A R . C O U N C I L . G O T
A G A P E . (S) C E N T . O T S
M Y N A . (P) H I . (K) H Z
S U C C (O) R I N G . (O) I L S
. (K) A A . G U T . (P) Y N E
I H E (A) R Y A . N I L S (S) O N
F O R G E T S . S E A B O R G
S P E E D O S . S T Y L E S
```

L	A	C	T	O		F	I	S	T	S		A	D	A	L	E
A	L	A	I	N		O	F	T	H	E		D	R	I	E	D
T	E	P	E	E		S	H	R	E	D		M	A	R	C	O
E	X	E	R	C	I	S	E	O	F	A	R	I	G	H	T	
R	A	T	R	A	C	E		B	E	R	E	T		E	U	R
			A	R	E		M	E	D	I	A		D	A	R	N
A	M	P			D	O	E			S	P	E	E	D	E	R
R	O	A	R	S		P	R	E	P		E	N	L			
P	O	W	E	R	M	A	Y	D	E	P	R	I	V	E	M	E
			E	T	C		L	U	R	E		D	E	M	O	S
F	U	N	F	A	C	T			P	A	D			U	P	C
O	N	E	S		R	O	O	T	S		A	B	U			
B	L	T		C	A	R	L	O		S	L	U	R	P	E	E
	O	F	T	H	E	R	I	G	H	T	I	T	S	E	L	F
C	O	L	O	R		E	V	I	T	A		M	I	L	E	R
I	S	I	T	I		N	E	V	E	R		O	N	E	N	O
S	E	X	E	S		T	R	E	N	T		M	E	G	A	N

B	E	B	E		L	I	N		P	O	M	P		M	I	A
L	A	R	D		L	A	U	R	E	N	C	E		I	S	H
T	R	A	Y	V	O	N	M	A	R	T	I	N		N	O	M
		I	S	A	Y		B	R	I	O		A	N	I	T	A
P	U	N		I	D	A		I	O	U	S		A	B	O	U
A	S	W	A	N		S	A	N	D	R	A	B	L	A	N	D
L	E	A	N		C	P	U				F	L	A	R	E	
M	U	S	T		H	E	L	L		C	E	O				
	P	H	I	L	A	N	D	O	C	A	S	T	I	L	E	
				A	S	S		N	O	N	E		C	O	A	L
	S	C	A	N	T				P	A	X		E	G	G	O
G	E	O	R	G	E	F	L	O	Y	D		S	T	R	E	P
L	A	M	E		N	A	A	N		A	D	O		O	R	E
A	T	B	A	T		C	H	O	O		A	B	E	L		
S	T	U		B	R	E	O	N	N	A	T	A	Y	L	O	R
E	L	S		S	H	I	R	E	L	L	E		R	E	P	O
R	E	T		P	E	T	E		Y	E	S		E	R	I	C

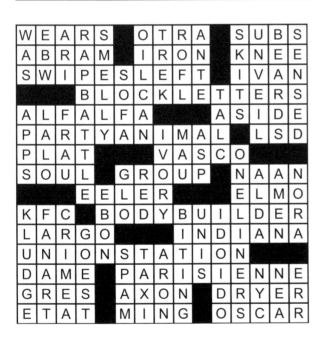

W	E	A	R	S		O	T	R	A		S	U	B	S
A	B	R	A	M		I	R	O	N		K	N	E	E
S	W	I	P	E	S	L	E	F	T		I	V	A	N
		B	L	O	C	K	L	E	T	T	E	R	S	
A	L	F	A	L	F	A				A	S	I	D	E
P	A	R	T	Y	A	N	I	M	A	L		L	S	D
P	L	A	T				V	A	S	C	O			
S	O	U	L		G	R	O	U	P		N	A	A	N
			E	E	L	E	R				E	L	M	O
K	F	C		B	O	D	Y	B	U	I	L	D	E	R
L	A	R	G	O				I	N	D	I	A	N	A
U	N	I	O	N	S	T	A	T	I	O	N			
D	A	M	E		P	A	R	I	S	I	E	N	N	E
G	R	E	S		A	X	O	N		D	R	Y	E	R
E	T	A	T		M	I	N	G		O	S	C	A	R

D	A	P		R	O	O	M	B	A		R	P	M	S
E	S	E		H	A	R	A	S	S		E	L	O	I
C	H	A	R	I	T	Y	R	A	P		V	A	N	S
I	P	H	O	N	E	X			E	R	I	C		
L	I	E	S	O	N		L	O	N	E	V	I	C	E
E	T	N	A			A	A	H		N	A	D	A	L
S	S	S		S	I	L	I	C	O	N	L	O	A	M
				E	C	O		O	W	E				
B	A	H	R	A	I	N	P	O	S	T		N	G	O
S	H	O	A	L		S	E	L			C	O	O	P
E	N	E	M	Y	H	O	G		T	U	T	T	U	T
		D	O	S	E			C	A	N	N	O	L	I
E	B	O	N		I	T	A	L	I	C	S	P	A	M
B	O	W	E		S	U	D	O	K	U		E	S	A
B	A	N	S		T	E	A	P	O	T		N	H	L

Grid 1 (top-left)

N	A	R	C		M	A	R	E		C	L	A	N	G
Y	S	E	R		E	D	E	N		U	S	U	A	L
M	Y	N	A		A	H	A	B		B	U	T	N	O
P	O	T	S	A	N	D	P	A	N	S		O	O	P
H	U	S	H	E	D		S	N	A	F	U			
		R	E	O		C	H	A	B	L	I	S		
C	A	R	H	O	R	N	S		S	N	O	O	D	S
O	L	E	O		E	A	T		A	L	I	T		
O	V	I	N	E	S		W	H	I	S	T	L	E	S
T	A	N	K	C	A	R		O	L	E				
	S	O	R	E	R		L	A	K	O	T	A		
B	A	M		C	A	C	E	R	O	L	A	Z	O	S
O	M	A	N	I		A	T	O	M		P	O	S	H
O	I	L	E	D		L	I	M	E		O	N	C	E
M	E	L	E	E		L	E	A	N		W	E	A	N

Grid 2 (top-right)

O	R	A	L		T	R	A	P	P	E	D		S	T	A	Y
S	O	S	O		R	E	C	L	I	N	E		T	H	R	O
C	O	S	T		E	Q	U	A	L	L	I	B	E	R	T	Y
A	M	I	S	S		R	T	E		F	R	O	Y	O		
R	B	G		W	H	E	A	T		O	N	L	O	W		
	A	N	T	I	E	S	S	E	N	T	I	A	L	I	S	M
	O	P	I	E		E	A	S	T		N	E	A			
S	C	A	R	E	S		S	E	A	R		A	G	N	I	
P	O	S	T	S	T	R	U	C	T	U	R	A	L	I	S	M
I	P	S	E		O	T	O	H		O	P	I	N	E	S	
E	S	O		S	C	A	R		A	H	A	B				
D	E	C	E	N	T	R	A	L	I	Z	A	T	I	O	N	
	I	R	O	N	S		O	R	O	N	O		N	O	M	
G	U	A	N	O		N	I	K		W	A	L	L	E		
A	N	T	I	P	O	L	I	T	I	C	S		R	I	O	T
I	D	E	E		D	A	T	E	N	U	T		O	N	O	R
T	O	S	S		E	M	E	R	G	E	S		N	E	K	O

Grid 3 (bottom-left)

D	S	M		S	E	A	W	A	Y	S		M	E	G
O	P	A		C	A	M	E	L	O	T		U	V	A
M	I	S	S	I	S	S	A	U	G	A		S	I	T
I	R	A	I	S	E		M	I	R	A	C	L	E	
N	E	L	L		L	O	O	N		E	L	O		
O	S	A	K	A		P	R	I	G		A	G	U	A
	M	E	A	D		A	R	R	E	S	T			
A	C	K	N	O	W	L	E	D	G	E	M	E	N	T
A	R	I	O	S	E		R	O	A	N				
S	U	I	T		S	L	I	T		T	R	I	E	S
	K	I	T		A	N	E	W		I	N	L	A	
A	L	A	T	E	E	N		I	C	O	N	I	C	
L	I	P		N	A	C	O	T	C	H	T	A	N	K
O	S	O		O	V	E	R	I	C	E		T	O	E
E	P	I		R	E	T	R	E	A	T		E	R	R

Grid 4 (bottom-right)

E	S	M	E		O	B	J	E	C	T		S	E	W
D	A	M	P		N	A	E	N	A	E		M	I	R
U	N	C	H	A	I	N	E	D	M	E	L	O	D	Y
C	E	L	E	B		H	R	S		M	O	R	E	L
	M	A	A	M		W	I	N	E	R	Y			
F	R	E	E	T	H	I	N	K	I	N	G			
L	O	W	R	E	S		G	A	N	G		B	B	L
I	K	E	A		P	R	Y		S	L	U	E		
M	U	S		I	D	E	A		E	N	T	E	R	S
	U	N	T	A	M	E	D	Y	O	U	T	H		
B	E	A	S	T	S		D	A	M	N				
A	L	B	E	E		L	E	G		P	E	A	R	L
W	I	L	D	G	O	O	S	E	C	H	A	S	E	S
D	D	E		E	D	W	A	R	D		G	I	G	A
Y	E	R		R	E	S	I	S	T		E	A	S	T

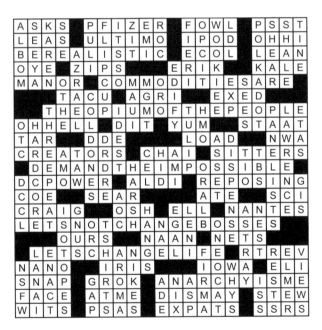

Top-left grid:

```
B U M . B A H . T Z U . J O T
I N A O N E P A I R . U N O
O R R O N R A M P S . S O Y
N U C L E A R R P L A N T .
I L I A D . T A O . I A M S
C Y A N . A M I . C A S S I O
. S P E C S . L E E K S .
T I C K E T I O F F I C E .
F O R A Y . A P N E A .
G R O C E R . A Y E . T A C O
S E N T . E A T . S A L A H
. C I G A R I F A C T O R Y
A C H . A L T O O N A . H B O
B A E . T L I N G I T . A O K
S P F . E Y E . S L S . S N O
```

Top-right grid:

```
M E N . S H O A L S . S C A N
A V E M A L L E T . A R C O
J A G G E D E D G E . M A I M
S C A L A . S A G E T . D D E
. T E R M . O P H E L I A
A S I A . A R C . E R E C T
F R O N T I E R T O W N .
T I N . R E T E A C H . C O Y
. B O R D E R C O L L I E
R E C A P . D O A . Y E L P
A G R E E T O . M E R V .
P G A . S A M S A . S I E N A
P E N S . P A C I F I C R I M
E R I E . A N A L O G . A L I
L S A T . S I T S O N . T E D
```

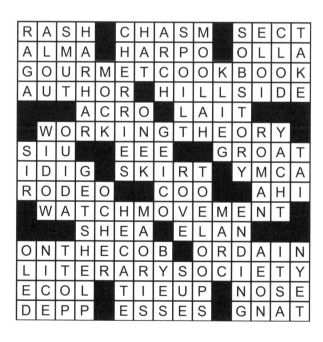

Bottom-left grid:

```
R A S H . C H A S M . S E C T
A L M A . H A R P O . O L L A
G O U R M E T C O O K B O O K
A U T H O R . H I L L S I D E
. A C R O . L A I T .
W O R K I N G T H E O R Y
S I U . E E E . G R O A T
I D I G . S K I R T . Y M C A
R O D E O . C O O . A H I
W A T C H M O V E M E N T .
. S H E A . E L A N .
O N T H E C O B . O R D A I N
L I T E R A R Y S O C I E T Y
E C O L . T I E U P . N O S E
D E P P . E S S E S . G N A T
```

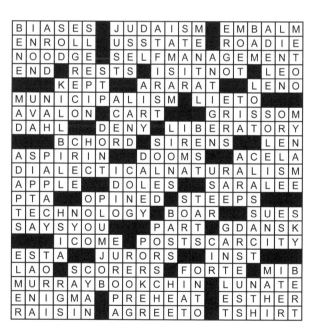

Bottom-right grid:

```
B I A S E S . J U D A I S M . E M B A L M
E N R O L L . U S S T A T E . R O A D I E
N O O D G E . S E L F M A N A G E M E N T
E N D . R E S T S . I S I T N O T . L E O
. K E P T . A R A R A T . L E N O
M U N I C I P A L I S M . L I E T O .
A V A L O N . C A R T . G R I S S O M
D A H L . D E N Y . L I B E R A T O R Y
. B C H O R D . S I R E N S . L E N
A S P I R I N . D O O M S . A C E L A
D I A L E C T I C A L N A T U R A L I S M
A P P L E . D O L E S . S A R A L E E
P T A . O P I N E D . S T E E P S .
T E C H N O L O G Y . B O A R . S U E S
S A Y S Y O U . P A R T . G D A N S K
. I C O M E . P O S T S C A R C I T Y
E S T A . J U R O R S . I N S T .
L A O . S C O R E R S . F O R T E . M I B
M U R R A Y B O O K C H I N . L U N A T E
E N I G M A . P R E H E A T . E S T H E R
R A I S I N . A G R E E T O . T S H I R T
```

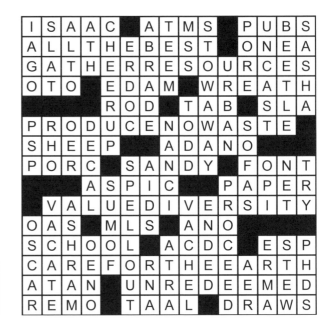

A	T	T	U		P	A	C	E	S		P	I	P	E
S	E	A	N		E	R	A	T	O		A	S	E	A
I	A	M	F	R	E	E	F	R	O	M	W	H	A	T
A	S	S	A	U	L	T		E	T	O	N			
			I	D	E	O				R	E	A	D	
I	A	M	R	I	D	O	F	O	W	N	E	R	O	F
R	A	U	L				L	A	W	S		M	M	I
I	T	S	Y		W	H	A	T	I		G	O	I	N
S	E	T		S	O	A	K				R	U	N	E
H	A	V	E	I	N	M	Y	P	O	W	E	R	O	R
	M	E	A	N				E	D	I	E			
			S	A	S	H		T	E	E	N	A	G	E
W	H	A	T	I	C	A	N	C	O	N	T	R	O	L
D	O	N	E		A	V	I	A	N		E	A	R	L
S	P	A	R		N	E	S	T	S		A	L	E	E

I	S	A	A	C		A	T	M	S		P	U	B	S
A	L	L	T	H	E	B	E	S	T		O	N	E	A
G	A	T	H	E	R	R	E	S	O	U	R	C	E	S
O	T	O		E	D	A	M		W	R	E	A	T	H
				R	O	D		T	A	B		S	L	A
P	R	O	D	U	C	E	N	O	W	A	S	T	E	
S	H	E	E	P			A	D	A	N	O			
P	O	R	C		S	A	N	D	Y		F	O	N	T
			A	S	P	I	C			P	A	P	E	R
	V	A	L	U	E	D	I	V	E	R	S	I	T	Y
O	A	S		M	L	S		A	N	O				
S	C	H	O	O	L		A	C	D	C		E	S	P
C	A	R	E	F	O	R	T	H	E	E	A	R	T	H
A	T	A	N		U	N	R	E	D	E	E	M	E	D
R	E	M	O		T	A	A	L		D	R	A	W	S

M	E	S	A	S		G	A	D	S		M	E	T	A
A	G	A	V	E		O	H	I	O		E	R	I	K
P	A	G	A	N		G	E	E	S		D	A	D	A
P	L	A	N	T	C	O	M	M	U	N	I	T	Y	
			T	O	I	L	S		E	A	T			
A	D	R	I	F	T			A	M	H	A	R	I	C
B	E	E		F	I	G	U	R	E	S	T	U	D	Y
A	C	T	S			A	L	T			E	P	I	C
F	O	R	M	F	I	T	T	I	N	G		E	N	L
T	R	O	I	L	U	S			A	L	L	E	G	E
			R	E	S		H	A	N	O	I			
	G	E	N	D	E	R	E	Q	U	A	L	I	T	Y
S	I	L	O		D	E	L	A		T	I	M	E	R
E	N	U	F		T	O	M	B		E	T	H	E	L
W	O	L	F		O	S	S	A		R	H	O	D	Y

D	S	T		G	O	D	E	L		N	O	M	A	R
I	C	H		I	N	A	W	E		B	L	I	G	E
S	H	E	L	T	E	R	E	D		C	A	R	O	L
	M	W	A	H		K	N	O	B		N	A	N	A
M	E	E	T	U	P			F	R	Y		N	I	X
B	A	S	E	B	A	L	L	F	I	E	L	D	S	
A	R	T			R	I	O		S	T	E	A	M	
			K	R	O	P	O	T	K	I	N			
	S	T	E	I	N		F	I	E			A	R	E
	C	A	N	D	Y	F	A	C	T	O	R	I	E	S
S	H	O		A	M	E			S	H	O	R	T	S
L	O	I	S		S	N	I	P		I	S	P	Y	
O	L	S	E	N		W	O	R	K	S	H	O	P	S
M	A	T	E	Y		A	T	A	L	E		D	E	I
O	R	S	A	Y		Y	A	Y	M	E		S	D	S

Grid 1

```
A B S . C H A W . L Y R I C
L O O P . L O S E . A C U R A
I N F O . A R A B . M A D A M
B U I L D S U P . G E M I N I
I S A I A [S/H] S . A R S E . .
. . C D S . F L A T R A T E
H A V E . O C U L I . P A I X
A C A I . C A B I N . U R G E
L E N D . I N A N Y . S P E D
F R E E B E E R . B A E . .
. . N I T S . R E D T A P E
C H A T T Y . F A N Z I N E S
P U R I M . W A N D . H A N S
A G I T A . E D G E . W I N E
P O L Y P . D E E R . S E X
```

Grid 2

```
E D O M . B U S S T O P . O G R E
L I N E . U N I C O R N . P L U M
F E E D . C E R A M I C . T U B E
I P S O S . R N C . T I E I N
S P I C E T E A . A B D U C T E D
H E E . M I C H . T R O D . O S S
. P I C A . A G E S .
E C I G . T R E K K I E . U C S F
L O R D . A D D E N D A . R O L E
I C O N I C . E G O . T H E C U T
A O C . A T A N . T A D A . K E A
S O N S . S H O W .
T I C K E T . E G G C U P
L E S E . S C R U M . I S I N
I T A L I C . L I P . C Y R A N O
B R I L L O . O C D . L U C I T E
S A D I S T . G E O . E L E N A S
```

Grid 3

```
S T A T S . H O T T U B . S P L I T
A R T E L . A S I A G O . A L O N E
N O R E A L S O C I A L C H A N G E
S T I N K A T . G R I N G O S
. H A S E V E R C O M E A B O U T .
. S N O B B E R Y .
R E S T S . M E I R . R A S T A
W I T H O U T A R E V O L U T I O N
A L A D D I N . R A I M E N T
N E R . S E T T L E D O W N . V E E
D E E D . A A B A . I E D S
A N A R C H I S M W H A T I T
. S T Y L U S . B U N S E N
R E A L L Y S T A N D S F O R
S E G U E . A I O L I S . R A I T A
S W A N S . N A D I N E . A F L A C
T E R S E . D R A P E S . G E E S E
```

FRIENDS OF AK PRESS

AK Press is small, in terms of staff and resources, but we also manage to be one of the world's most productive anarchist publishing houses. We publish close to twenty books every year, and distribute thousands of other titles published by like-minded independent presses and projects from around the globe. We're entirely worker run and democratically managed. We operate without a corporate structure—no boss, no managers, no bullshit.

The Friends of AK program is a way you can directly contribute to the continued existence of AK Press, and ensure that we're able to keep publishing books like this one! Friends pay $25 a month directly into our publishing account ($30 for Canada, $35 for international), and receive a copy of every book AK Press publishes for the duration of their membership! Friends also receive a discount on anything they order from our website or buy at a table: 50 percent on AK titles, and 30 percent on everything else. We have a Friends of AK e-book program as well: $15 a month gets you an electronic copy of every book we publish for the duration of your membership. You can even sponsor a deeply discounted membership for someone in prison.

Email friendsofak@akpress.org for more info, or visit the website: akpress.org/friends.html.

There are always great book projects in the works—so sign up now to become a Friend of AK Press, and let the presses roll!